9-29-72

Gather

GATHER UP THE FRAGMENTS is a modern man's conversation with God— but a distinctly different kind of conversation. One that is relaxed, contemplative, personal—and friendly. One in which God is not thought of as transcendent, far off, detached or vengeful, but as *real*, a "close-up God."

there is no hidden treasure chest of miracles to give us the sense of God's realness . . . but in the endless proliferation of trivia within today's consumer paradise . . . we can still find amid all the hawking . . . quiet and seemingly harmless statements that are actually revolutionary explosives . . . like "I have come that they may have life" . . .

Life—in the Trinity within man, in his own ordinariness and his extraordinariness, in his understanding of God not as "the Grand Extortioner of the cloudlands" but as loving, intimate and real—is what GATHER UP THE FRAGMENTS is "about." But it is also about how we deal with others, how we judge them and how we injure them both with what we say and what we fail to say, what we do and what we fail to do, failing to recognize our mutual identity—that "Christ-I" and "Christ-they" are really "Christ-we," united by a central truth

. . . that will pull in all our fragmented truths and beliefs . . . a synthesis . . . the Trinity within us . . . is the truth into which we can gather up the fragments. . . .

Gather Up
the Fragments

by T. R. HANEY

Sheed and Ward · New York

Copyright © by SHEED AND WARD, INC., 1971
Library of Congress Catalog Card Number: 72-162381
Standard Book Number: 8362-1196-0

Manufactured in the United States of America

1713300

Contents

v

Gather Up the Fragments

Introduction

God is "dead" precisely because he has so long been thought of as transcendent . . . far off . . . detached . . . even vengeful . . . to be sure, he created all things good . . . but that was long ago . . . men have corrupted the original good . . . so today, in their agnostic anxiety, they need massive doses of a close-up God . . . they need to experience the realness of God. . . .

there is no hidden treasure chest of miracles to give us this sense of God's realness . . . but in the endless proliferation of trivia within today's consumer paradise . . . we can still find amid all the hawking . . . quiet and seemingly harmless statements that are actually revolutionary explosives . . . like "I have come that they may have *life*" . . . as a matter of historical fact, these explosives have been detonated . . . but we've learned to live with the debris. . . .

if modern man is honest . . . he will go out among
the civilized wreckage and gather up the fragments. . . .

even those who do not think of God as the Grand
Extortioner of the cloudlands . . . must pause . . . for
perhaps he has become something even worse for
them . . . a "thing" . . . and perhaps their frenzied
spiritual efforts are but imitative grotesqueries of
the original "good news" . . . perhaps their life,
called Christian, is dulled by the insensitive
complacencies of routine piety . . . and because they
have been so busy fulfilling the letter of the law . . .
they, too, need to experience the realness of God . . .
personal . . . loving . . . intimate. . . .

if modern Christians are honest . . . whether in the
world . . . or called into the precincts of religious
dedication . . . they will take inventory . . . to see if
they have not put their Christianity into neat and
reassuring compartments . . . and if they have . . .
they, too, will go among their prized packages . . .
and gather up the fragments. . . .

what a great need we have today . . . of a depthful
consciousness . . . a vibrant realization . . . a keen
awareness . . . of what we already know but seldom
advert to . . . the difference among people . . . is the
difference of depth and surface . . . and we are all
in need of an ever-deepening faith . . . so that we will

genuinely appreciate (in all the literalness of that
word) . . . what we say we believe in. . . .

what we need is a centripetal truth . . . that will pull
in all our fragmented truths and beliefs . . . a
synthesis . . . the Trinity within us . . . is the truth
into which we can gather up the fragments. . . .

Trinity Within Me

I am told, God, that You, Father, Son and Spirit . . .
actually and really live . . . within me . . . I've heard
it before . . . read it somewhere . . . call it moral
lassitude, if You will . . . or maybe it's been crammed
into a nook of an overstuffed and carefully disarrayed
memory . . . but, for me, this theory of what is called
the "Divine Indwelling" . . . has been, if anything,
translated haltingly and monosyllabically . . . into
practice. . . .

I don't want to pass the buck . . . but your being
within me certainly hasn't been propounded too
often . . . or too clearly . . . I can't say that I've been
told very much about it . . . in the foreboding
rhetoric of the pulpit . . . or in the whispered counsels
of the confessional . . . it seems I've been warned of
my obligations . . . accused of my failings . . . isolated
virtues have been presented for me to acquire . . .
texts from scripture have been used as springboards . . .

for some tirade . . . all in all it hasn't been a very
personal experience . . . sort of a Prussian exposition
on discipline . . . not too much warmth . . . or too
terribly encouraging . . . (I hate to be critical but this
indwelling *was* passed over rather superficially . . .)
my religious education . . . again announced my
duties . . . painted sufferings for sin in gloomy
colors . . . and You, God, emerged as the Divine
Executioner, I'm afraid . . . if it hadn't been for Jesus
Christ's death . . . no telling what your anger might
have done to us . . . your anger, too, was presented
as being rather whimsical . . . I could never quite
figure out what stoked the fires of your anger . . . in
the first place . . . against *me* . . . when your love
was mentioned . . . it seemed far distant . . . and like
the final payoff reserved for the eternal later . . .
once I had been cleared at the celestial bench of
justice . . . I think all the while . . . down deep . . .
I wanted your love . . . reassurance of your love . . .
so You can see that your indwelling strikes me as
strange . . . and foreign. . . .

now I'm told not to "say prayers" . . . but to
converse . . . naturally . . . to be familiar . . . relaxed . . .
like one of the family . . . *that* kind of "belonging" . . .
with You . . . the infinite God . . . awesome . . . and
all-powerful . . . the ominous God of Abraham,
Isaac and Jacob . . . Speaker from the clouds . . .
whose echo chamber is thunder . . . at whose voice . . .
Peter, James and John . . . fell flat on their faces. . . .

of *course*, I hesitate . . . I object . . . I haven't been
trained that way . . . You were the One who would
punish me . . . if I even "talked in church" . . . I
confessed it . . . it was a sin . . . I was trained (so
well) . . . to be meticulously respectful . . . when
I came into God's presence . . . now your presence
is within me? . . . and I'm supposed to be comfortable
with You? . . . I feel as though I should hold my
breath! . . . so I'm told to mature religiously . . . to
reexamine some basic concepts . . . like Grace . . .
a "gift" . . . I know that . . . but a gift of what? . . .
something You share, happy Trinity, with us . . .
through your Christ . . . and mine . . . a gift in the
form of a transfusion . . . it begins to seem almost
irritatingly obvious . . . but I can't get myself to
conclude. . . .

a transfusion of your life . . . the infinite God's life! . . .
"I have come that they may have life and have
it abundantly" . . . I guess this statement of Christ's
never meant much to me. . . .

I've never thought much . . . about your presence . . .
your intimacy . . . your activity . . . in me . . .
what a love You must have for us! . . . a genuine
home-love . . . You, the boundless . . . omnipotent . . .
all-present . . . eternal . . . immense God . . . within
me . . . I can hardly imagine . . . so I must believe . . .
I certainly do need a mature faith . . . for this. . . .

Smug Satisfaction

The more I consider . . . my indwelling God . . . the
fact that You are in me . . . the more real You
become . . . the simpler everything seems . . . I have
been vacillating . . . between momentary interest . . .
and periods of easily deflated enthusiasm . . . when
I don't remember . . . your presence within me . . . I
have more time to calculate my many invaluable
achievements . . . in my own personal life of
piety . . . but when You exert the pressure of your
indwelling . . . all my efforts seem like wheels
grinding out sawdust. . . .

it's the strangest realization . . . that these labyrinthine
devotions of mine . . . which keep me flitting . . . like
a bee in a flowerbed . . . seem to serve only to make
me lose my way to You . . . what a shock . . . all these
devotions . . . yet I seem to have forgotten *You* . . .
sometimes I wonder . . . if I've really ever *known*
You . . . perhaps I've been more devoted to my

devotions than to You . . . weaving a web of multiplied
words . . . I don't really want to admit this . . . it
would seem like so much wasted time . . . yet You
do look at good will . . . and weigh efforts . . . and
You want me, at this point, to enter into a more
personal relationship . . . with You . . . within me . . .
"this people honors me with its lips" . . . could this
have been my attitude? . . .

there have been times . . . when I've put myself on
a schedule of prayer . . . or had to follow one . . .
and fulfilled it . . . "getting in" this prayer . . . or that
devotion . . . the prayer-book tradition . . . yes, I
had to "get my prayers in" . . . yet, when I'm brutally
honest with myself . . . I think I actually failed to
realize *why* . . . I was "getting in" all those
prayers . . . something vague about being holier . . .
or a preservative from falling into sin . . . a sort of
Christian phylactery . . . now when I look back . . .
it all seems so self-centered . . . there was the smug
feeling of satisfaction . . . even of self-righteousness . . .
because I had "said" all my prayers . . . followed
my schedule . . . and You, Three Persons, were living
within me . . . all the time . . . "they have had their
reward". . . .

schedules of prayer are certainly wonderful helps . . .
but so often . . . they become the essence . . . as
though without them . . . you couldn't be holy. . . .

the Sabbath was made for man . . . and not the other way around . . . and all the time . . . You were within me. . . .

good habits of prayer . . . yes . . . but what about the habitual remembrance of your presence? . . .

was it sadly ludicrous . . . to watch me get all my prayers in? . . . to see the feverish activity of my personal efforts? . . . while I forgot You . . . or at most thought of You . . . as "way up there" . . . on your throne . . . flattered by what I was doing for You. . . .

your indwelling . . . demands that I become conscious of You . . . and not just be complacent . . . about going through the formality . . . of private and public ritual . . . your indwelling . . . demands that my prayer . . . be an experience of You . . . I must be present to You . . . the more I try to realize your presence within me . . . the less energy I'll have for patting my own efforts on the back. . . .

The Insecurity of God

These are strange times . . . Trinity within me . . .
times of change . . . times of bewilderment . . .
tumultuous times . . . uncertain times . . . times of
careless criticism . . . and frightened dogmatism . . .
of sophisticated disdain . . . and frivolous disregard . . .
times of insecurity . . . problems: who ever thought
we'd be hearing celibacy being decried? . . . or birth
control being disputed? . . . or religious life being
criticized as irrelevant? . . . everything we held near
and dear . . . seems to be under attack . . . some
things are even scoffed at . . . and even when I accept
changes intellectually . . . I wonder if I'm emotionally
prepared . . . I find myself asking . . . what was
wrong with the way things were? . . . were we less
fervent? . . . less prayerful? . . . less Christian? . . .

one thing for sure . . . we weren't less secure . . .
O God! . . . the strength of that security . . . and
yet . . . I think I have to admit . . . I wasn't particularly
conscious . . . of You . . .within me . . . Father . . .

13

Son . . . Spirit . . . God . . . I mean really conscious . . .
habitually . . . yet it's a fact that You are within
us . . . "this is how we know he lives in us: by the
Spirit whom he has given us" . . . to know . . . and
to be aware of . . . there *is* a difference . . .
awareness means absorbing knowledge . . . we were
fervent, prayerful, Christian . . . but perhaps on a
superficial level . . . life is not superficial . . .
self-preservation is of fundamental concern . . . not
something you take or leave . . . "He told us this
truth that God has given us everlasting life" . . . in
all our fervor and prayers and Christian living . . .
how appreciative have we been . . . of this life in
us . . . that is everlasting? . . . perhaps we've associated
"everlasting" with the other side of the grave . . . and
yet, Grace is the beginning of Glory . . . now . . .
what more do I need for security? . . .

maybe this nostalgia for the security of times past . . .
is due to the fact that it was based on me . . . "me"
is very concrete . . . my actions . . . are fairly easy to
perceive. . . and analyze . . . but when I deal with
You . . . infinite and incomprehensible . . . "God's
ways are not ours" . . . maybe there's no
measure for security . . . and this frightens me . . .
or perhaps I'm afraid . . . that a love-involvement
with You . . . will be more demanding . . . the
mechanical procedures of my acts . . . sometimes
don't even require my attention . . . You do . . . and
being in your presence . . . consciously . . . demands

more of me . . . than praying in the market place of
my own conscience. . . .

maybe when I do converse with You . . . about
ordinary things . . . the children . . . work . . . life and
sickness . . . boredom . . . You become so real for
me . . . so close . . . that I want to run . . . before, when
I "prayed" . . . perhaps I was talking only to
myself . . . with a semiconscious feeling . . . that You
were somehow included . . . You're too much for
me . . . I can't fake it . . . I liked it better, I think, when
You were far away . . . then you didn't bother me . . .
I wasn't too aware that You were actually listening
to me . . . now that I'm becoming more conscious
of You within me . . . and my prayer is just an
ordinary . . . everyday conversation . . . well, "who
can see God and live?" . . . your very realness that I
want to experience . . . shakes me. . . .

I feel joy . . . and fright . . . peace . . . and chaos . . .
my God . . . Trinity within me . . . it's just too
much . . . yours is a paradoxical security . . . but yours
is what I want . . . and desperately. . . .

Mediocrity

When I think it over . . . in rare, honest moments . . .
Father, Son and Spirit within me . . . my finely
structured existence: "now I work . . . now I play . . .
now I pray" . . . skillfully compartmentalized . . .
has actually kept me . . . away from You . . . at least
from an experienced intimacy. . . .

everything was so pat . . . so neat . . . so orderly . . .
so businesslike . . . I did my share (merit) . . . and
You did yours (grace) . . . no disturbance . . . no
uneasiness . . . no real inconvenience . . . it's not even
like asking . . . for a sign . . . it's giving yourself
the sign . . . now I'm Christian . . . now I'm not. . . .

"be hot or cold" . . . but because you are lukewarm? . . .
I guess that's it . . . I've been mediocre . . . actually
a miracle worker . . . producing fruit from thorns . . .
even when I made what I thought was heroic effort . . .
I was just being smug . . . claiming to have nowhere
to lay my head . . . but foxy enough to keep around

a spare den . . . "I have come to cast fire upon the
earth" . . . what strange words . . . no need for that . . .
the world has become civilized . . . sophisticated . . .
it doesn't hate you because you want to "practice
your religion" . . . not anymore. . . .

yet, Spirit within me . . . You are a wind . . . that
stirs . . . and disturbs . . . a fire that burns . . . and
destroys . . . destroys all the "me" . . . knocks
down my exquisitely wrought compartments . . .
melts together the steel walls of my studied
schizophrenia. . . .

this "renewal" isn't outside me . . . as though I
could stand back and watch it . . . detached . . . it's
going on within me . . . and within others, too . . .
and forcing itself out into the whole Body . . . the
more aware I am of your indwelling . . . eternal
Three . . . the less complacent I can be . . . I'm upset . . .
not because the renewal . . . is making me lose my
faith . . . it's shaking it . . . awake . . . what I *am*
losing is my complacency . . . and this annoys me . . .
because complacency is so restful . . . so tidy . . .
so unperturbing . . . complacency means . . .
that I can live my Christian life . . . according to
high-sounding but vague generalites . . . complacency
breeds comfortable mediocrity. . . .

but the growing experience . . . of You within me . . .
challenges my self-satisfying mediocrity. . . .

18

I talk about being in the "state of grace" . . . translated
into meaningful language . . . that means God's life
is in me . . . but God's life isn't a thing . . . it's a
Person . . . the Third Person . . . so if I'm in the state
of grace . . . I have Life in me . . . realizing this . . .
how could I possibly be mediocre? . . . "if we live by
the Spirit, let us also follow the Spirit" . . . life isn't
static . . . it moves . . . grows . . . do I have a choice? . . .
mustn't I follow the Spirit? . . . actively . . . because
You are within me . . . doesn't mean that I'll be
lulled . . . into passivity . . . I must be active . . . but
my activity . . . must be directed by You . . . my
indwelling God . . . all my own efforts can be of
benefit to me . . . only when I live . . . in the pervasive
context . . . of You within me. . . .

Spiritual Exercises

As I become more vividly aware of your presence . . .
within me . . . my Christian living becomes more
simplified . . . and this continual preoccupation with
You, happy Trinity . . . raises a question . . . why
do I have to stop conversing with You . . . in order
to converse with You . . . at a specified time . . . in a
mapped-out manner . . . perhaps even in a definite
place? . . . in other words . . . what about the
structures . . . of the days . . . before I really
recognized You within me? . . . what are called
"spiritual exercises" . . . now they seem like artificial
arrangements . . . fastidiously attending to minutiae. . . .

the apostles were continually in the presence of
Christ . . . yet he told them . . . "come aside
awhile" . . . he himself spent long nights . . .
communicating . . . he who said: "the Father and
I are one" . . . as no one of us could say . . . and "as
the Father has life in himself, even so he has given
to the Son also to have life in himself" . . . yet he

21

kept going to the temple . . . "my Father's house" . . .
he called it. . . .

likewise these "spiritual exercises" . . . afford me
the opportunity . . . of pinpointing my consciousness
of You within me . . . they're opportunities for
undisturbed moments to be with You . . .
undistracted . . . the moment I place myself above
them . . . I begin to weaken my conscious
relationship . . . with You . . . "he who exalts
himself, shall be humbled" . . . these opportunities
need not be of the same ironclad formality as
before . . . nor should they be treated . . . as though
we haven't given You a thought . . . since the last
"exercise" . . . we'd be going right back to the
compartments . . . overformality can destroy the
spontaneity of love. . . .

actually, the habitual reference to You within me . . .
throughout the day . . . drives me to seek You
out . . . in concentrated communiques . . . particular
prayers . . . or devotions . . . or reading . . . or
meditative thoughts . . . as my vocation in life
demands. . . .

this consciousness of You within me . . . makes
me understand . . . more fully . . . the sheer
interpersonal relationship I have . . . with You . . .
in these "exercises" . . . so that they don't become
"things" . . . in themselves . . . but occasions . . . of

Three . . . are within me . . . and still be marked by
such desperate hopelessness? . . . I must be looking
to myself . . . for strength . . . *I* am still the center
of all my religious endeavors . . . I haven't even
begun to realize that my strength is Christ . . . haven't
started to plumb the depths of his words . . . "without
me, you can do nothing". . . .

furthermore . . . besides a self-sufficiency verging
on despair . . . I've associated holiness with
canonization . . . as though this were the only kind
of holiness . . . the moment I concede this position . . .
is the moment holiness is beyond my reach . . . I
won't think of canonization as my goal . . .
consciously . . . humility forbids it . . . but down
deep in the core . . . with whizzing fragments of the
lives of the saints . . . falling all around me . . .
what does holiness really mean . . . to me? . . . who
is in the center? . . .

moreover . . . it can often happen that holiness is
equated with . . . faultlessness . . . when this does
occur . . . holiness becomes an impossible ideal . . .
humanly . . . the goal which Christ has set . . .
decays . . . and holiness becomes propriety . . . a stern
propriety . . . that views Christ as a cold, martinet-like
commander . . . and my life . . . my Christian
living . . . is but evidence of icy moral rectitude . . .
"the just man falls seven times daily" . . . how then
this faultlessness? . . . again, *I* am the center. . . .

finally . . . I look at holiness as though it were
something to strive after . . . to seek out . . . to move
toward . . . something external . . . like a coat . . .
that I may eventually put on . . . if I keep all the
regulations . . . in reality . . . holiness is within
me . . . You came at baptism . . . to dwell within me . . .
You are holiness . . You shared yourself with me . . .
and so I was privileged to share in your holiness . . .
"before the world was made, he chose us, chose us
in Christ to be holy and spotless and to live through
love in his presence" . . . "to *be* holy". . . .

I was made holy . . . right from the start . . . changed
from being unholy . . . to being holy . . . radically . . .
this is why St. Paul can tell us . . . to "worship God
by offering your living bodies as a *holy* sacrifice" . . .
and he reminded the Roman converts . . . that
because as pagans they were brought the "good
news" . . . they had been "made holy by the Holy
Spirit" . . . so holiness . . . already exists in me . . .
it's just a matter of growth . . . all because of You . . .
eternal Three . . . because You have made me your
home . . . "you have been sanctified and become holy
because I am holy" . . . the mystery of holiness . . .
is the mystery of your indwelling. . . .

Transformation

Philosophers have tried to define You as "pure
activity" . . . and, therefore, since You dwell within
me . . . You must be doing something . . . *what* are
You doing? . . . sometimes, in an outburst of bourgeois
imaginings . . . I sort of think of You . . . as "sitting
around" . . . within me . . . twiddling your divine
thumbs . . . until the clarion call of eternity sounds
my turn . . . I realize, of course, that such a picture
is just a clownish display . . . of inaccuracy . . . it
takes no theological hairsplitting to know You are
doing something. . . .

"I live yet not I but Christ lives in me" . . . that's
it! . . . You are transforming me more and more into
Christ . . . and transformation is not some mount
of Transfiguration . . . which I'm climbing . . .
haltingly . . . transformation isn't a goal achieved
by external imitation . . . as though I had the Pelagian
task . . . of creating an imposing facade . . . called
Christ. . . .

transformation is something . . . that took place
initially . . . in baptism . . . and now must grow . . .
develop. . . .

we certainly miss a lot . . . we're superficial . . .
efficient? . . . our attitude toward religion . . . seems
always to have been . . . I do my share . . . and You
do yours . . . clinically scientific . . . Horn and
Hardart spirituality . . . I keep the rules . . . and
You *must* come across with my reward. . . .

then I show up in the swirling clouds of heaven . . .
and the angel audits my savings account book . . .
aren't You glad *I* did so much? . . . now reward me! . . .

there's knowledge that comes from business
dealings . . . there's knowledge that comes from
love . . . and I may find out that You're at most . . .
a business acquaintance of mine . . . but what
about all my efforts . . . prayers said . . . sacrifices
endured . . . sacraments received? . . . all a blunder? . . .
plotted with care and published with pomp? . . .
could it be possible . . . that by some ironic switch
of identity . . . after all my meritorious deeds . . .
You will see only *me* . . . and not Christ? . . .

my cooperation is certainly needed . . . but as a
condition . . . not as a substitute . . . for your action
within me . . . my efforts can never be . . . a royal

dismissal . . . of your creative activity within me . . .
it is You who transform me into Christ . . . so often
I transform your Christening activity . . . into the
"merits" of my punitive superego . . . is your
increasing . . . Christ . . . and my decreasing . . . to
be looked upon as a matter of poetic justice . . .
perpetrated by a sadistic God? . . . what a sickening
show of preoccupation with self! . . . and all the
while . . . You are within me. . . .

Growth in Identification

Growing up in You . . . Christ . . . that's what
Christianity is all about . . . in a day when so
many questions are being hurled at the "imperial
structure" . . . (and many legitimate ones) . . .
and when so many are wondering why they even
need . . . the "institution" . . . I'm afraid . . . God
within me . . . that the answers . . . in so many
instances . . . are nothing better than a legalized
hatchet job . . . with this difference . . . now they're
accompanied by a smile of pity . . . for the "lost" . . .
rather than the official furrowed brow of anger . . .
for the enemy . . . fundamental questions cannot be
answered with finely wrought trivia. . . .

growing up in You, Jesus . . . so obvious . . .
so fundamental . . . so little propounded . . .
Christ-identification . . . how little we think of
it . . . if I am a genuine follower of yours . . .
then my name is . . . "Christ-I" . . . this mystery . . .
is the launching pad . . . from which I blast off
into all the ramifications of Christian living . . . a

mystery . . . I've got to contemplate it . . . a lot . . .
in a quiet so alien to modern living. . . .

before I lodge all my questions . . . punctuated with
a condemnatory smirk . . . I've got to at least give
a fundamental like Christ-identification . . . the
benefit of the certainty. . . .

it's so easy to confront . . . a hatchet . . . with a
sledgehammer. . . .

maybe we should try using a ball and chain . . . on
our not so daring restlessness . . . settle down . . .
and think about a few fundamentals . . . they're
there to be thought over. . . .

all right . . . Trinity within me . . . You get pretty
tired and upset today . . . I'll grant this . . . legitimately
impatient . . . leadership may well be lacking . . .
implementation wanting . . . reaction stubborn . . .
but while I'm dug in at the wailing wall . . . how
much depthful thinking am I doing? . . . or if I'm
running through the streets crying wolf . . . maybe
I should sit down and catch my breath . . . on the
breathless. . . .

you can dissipate a lot of energy today . . . (that's
not what's meant by "freedom") . . . energy that could
be channeled into a very basic act of generosity . . .
giving myself over to You . . . indwelling God . . .
so that You . . . the Second Person made Man . . .

can assume me to yourself . . . identify me with
yourself . . . live another life on earth in and
through me. . . .

imagine: You, Christ, want to love others through
          me . . .
          You, Christ, want to help people in need . . .
          through me . . .
          You, Christ, want to heal . . . teach . . .
          pray . . . through *me*. . . .

and where am I? . . . busy . . . being feverishly
generous . . . in other ways . . . so urgently
generous . . . in saying my prayers . . . keeping
the laws . . . fulfilling my duties . . . avoiding sin . . .
running to the sacraments . . . working for the
renewal. . . .

so many *things* . . . for a generous person to do. . . .

and in my conscience-quieting . . . ego-feeding
frenzy . . . I really have no time for You . . . Christ . . .
just can't make room . . . You want to break into
my life . . . already swollen with enormous tasks for
You . . . this identification of You and me . . . will
have to take place . . . without my conscious effort . . .
I'm already exhausted . . . and I have an impressive
array of statistical data . . . to prove it . . . anyway
it's safer to do all these things . . . measurable . . .
I know what *I* have done . . . growing in identity
with You . . . too vague . . . can't be pinned down . . .

1713300

it's for mystics . . . I'm just ordinary . . . I'd better
make sure of my place . . . in purgatory . . . before
I aim at mysticism. . . .

yet . . . I've already admitted to You . . . eternal Three
within me . . . that holiness *is* for the ordinary . . .
am I back again to false dichotomies? . . . holiness . . .
transformation . . . identification . . . entirely
different? . . . as though I can be holy . . . without
being "Christ-I"? . . .

could it be that my pious practices . . . constitute a
door slamming in your face . . . Christ? . . . can my
understanding of the whole You . . . be so shallow . . .
that I can actually think I'm serving the "Church" . . .
while stunting my growth in You? . . .

while I'm running around . . . busy housecleaning
the bureaucratic pigeonholes . . . with my legitimate
complaints and honest criticisms . . . I may well end
up . . . on the dunghill of my own bitter desolation. . . .

I've much to think about . . . got to get away . . .
from compartmentalizations . . . my god . . . has so
often been . . . a bellyful of smug satisfaction . . .
because of all the good things I've done . . . indwelling
Trinity . . . I'm beginning to realize that I must
grow . . . in identification with Jesus Christ . . .
"who will refashion the body of our lowliness . . .
conforming it to the body of his glory". . . .

Others

There's another thought . . . eternal Trinity within
me . . . that has been dancing teasingly around the
vestibule of my consciousness . . . I feel kind of
excited about it . . . I'd like to pursue it . . . to see
where it leads. . . .

You're dwelling in me . . . but You're dwelling in
others, too! . . . I can't be sure . . . if You're in others
through grace . . . but I do know You're there through
your creative power . . . You know, if I bury
myself . . . all alone . . . in You within me . . . I
could end up just as smug and self-satisfied . . . as
when I was measuring all my fine efforts . . . on
your behalf . . . this, of course, is a much more subtle
self-centeredness . . . a mystical selfishness. . . .

being so preoccupied with You in me . . . in distant
isolation . . . and cold satisfaction . . . could make
me think I'm "somebody" . . . and like St. Paul says . . .
I'd just be deceiving myself . . . because that very

37

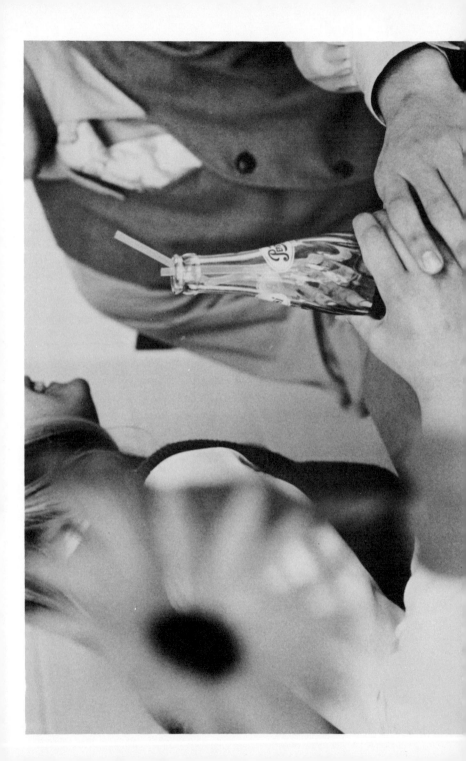

thought would prove I'm nobody . . . it's pure
perversion . . . I'm making a fool out of You . . .
taking your indwelling . . . a gift . . . and turning
it into a spotlight . . . on my own imperialist value . . .
self-styled. . . .

yet Christianity is sharing. . . .

so I must strengthen my consciousness . . . of You
within others . . . I have been indifferent to this
fact . . . (an indifference due not so much to personal
attitude . . . as to cultural happenstance) . . . either
way I can't excuse myself anymore . . . and while I
adore You within myself . . . I must adore You in
others . . . God within *us!* . . . what a grounds for
unity . . . "the wise peacemakers who go on quietly
sowing" . . . says St. James . . . "for a harvest of
righteousness *in other people* and in themselves" . . .
with this basic idea . . . a genuine harmony can
emerge . . . from the shoulder-bumping strife . . . that
occurs normally in human living. . . .

"never act from motives of rivalry . . . or personal
vanity" . . . You within *us* . . . what a motive for
sharing . . . for being truly Christian . . . for living
"together in love . . . as though you had only one
mind and one spirit between you". . . .

we look for bonds . . . to bind us together. . . .

communications . . . patriotism . . . space discovery . . .
scientific advancements . . . inventions . . . sociological
research . . . speedier transportation. . . .

yet as you go along . . . in your daily lockstep
routine . . . you know you're mentally ostracizing . . .
so many . . . waving the flag of your own personal
emancipation . . . from others . . . despite what the
researchers are contributing . . . to the forward-bound
evolution. . . .

the more we discover . . . to unite ourselves . . . the
more the isolation grows . . . it seems. . . .

yet we have turned the essential corner irreversibly . . .
long ago . . . is it so simple . . . that the complex
mechanism of our advanced civilization . . . just can't
absorb it? . . . "that they all may be one . . . just as
You, Father, live in me and I live in You . . . I am
asking that they may live in us . . . that they may be
one . . . as we are one" . . . it certainly wasn't for
your own benefit that You prayed . . . nor just for
ours . . . but as a *sign* even to our technologically
superior today . . . "that they may grow complete
into one . . . so that the world may realize". . . .

"look, World," we can say, "you're not getting the
job done . . . we have the answer . . . it's not just
a frozen dogmatic formulation . . . it's living truth . . .

pervasive . . . *God* dwells within *us* . . . can't we
start from here?" . . .

so often the World . . . is saying this . . . to us . . .
well, *I've* got to start from there, at least . . . I want
to grow in this consciousness . . . You in me . . . You
in others . . . Father . . . Son . . . Spirit . . . "partakers
of the divine nature," St. Peter tells us . . . now just
what does that mean? . . . sheer poetry? . . . or sheer
faith? . . . I opt for the latter . . . so I must work
toward the oneness of us all . . . by sharing . . . my
growing experience of You . . . with others. . . .

Involvement

There's something that's been bothering me . . .
about all this talk on involvement. . . .

sometimes you get the impression . . . that it's all a
fad . . . superficial . . . "trendy" . . . you're even
tempted to think that involvement . . . is some sort
of an orgy of philanthropy . . . Trinity within
me . . . marchers . . . assembly-line signers of
public petitions . . . ghetto workers . . . poverty
programmers . . . banner carriers . . . slogan makers . . .
inner city dwellers . . . all . . . human derricks
uplifting the underprivileged. . . .

the more you think about it, though, the more you
gradually begin to pin the difficulty down . . . and an
answer begins to emerge from the maze of distracted
thoughts . . . it's essential for the Christian to be
involved . . . in the needs of others . . . but Christian
involvement doesn't begin there . . . it begins with
You . . . indwelling Trinity . . . and returns to You . . .

only in this way can mere surface involvement . . .
mere fad-finding . . . mere veneer mission . . .
be avoided. . . .

we can't be involved . . . with man . . . without
God . . . or vice versa. . . .

it's not a case of "taking care" of all my religious
practices . . . nor is it a matter of pious poses . . .
nor pietistic monologues passed off as spiritual
conversations . . . and then with what time is left . . .
devoting myself to the needs of others. . . .

that would be artificial compartmentalization . . .
again . . . an historic schizophrenia . . . of forgetting
all else while trying to concentrate on You . . . or
forgetting You while trying to concentrate on all else
(i.e., works of love). . . .

baptism has made us integral . . . You introduced
yourself into our innermost being . . . then . . . as *the*
unifying force . . . compartments are unchristian . . .
schizophrenia . . . a disease . . . my pious practices
become "things" . . . and people become "things" . . .
I end up using them . . . (in the worst sense of the
word) . . . for my own stockpile of merit . . . God
within me . . . when will we ever learn . . . that "merit"
is not a miserly tabulation . . . of my calculated
investments . . . giving me an entree to eternal coupon
clipping? . . . merit . . . (as Louis Evely says) . . .

is the eternalizing of moments . . . things . . . and
beings we'd like to enjoy forever. . . .

it's only by remembering You within me . . . Father,
Son and Spirit . . . by experiencing You . . . by
realizing all that You're doing for me . . . that I can
begin to give myself . . . generously . . . selflessly . . .
to forget myself . . . inconvenience me . . . in order
to be involved with others. . . .

anyone intent on social witness . . . must be vibrantly
alive to You within him . . . and not just once in
a while. . . .

"that they all may be one in us" . . . what's the sense
of pouring ourselves out . . . like cement . . . to unite
everybody . . . if we're not going to be united in
You . . . in the consciousness of You? . . . without
You . . . without this consciousness . . . concerned
people are just so much stale putty . . . it falls out
with the first jarring crisis. . . .

You are still the alpha and omega . . . of Christian
involvement . . . and I can't say I love You . . . unless
I've shared my goods . . . with others . . . those in
need . . . of my time . . . energy . . . talents . . . joy . . .
optimism . . . hope . . . plans . . . ideals . . . dreams . . .
I can't approach You . . . if I'm nursing a grudge
against someone . . . anyone . . . it's You right within
me . . . who strengthens me so I can share . . . make

peace . . . cause happiness . . . dispel despair . . . so
that I can come to You . . . in order to return . . .
refreshed . . . revitalized . . . renewed . . . to more
sharing . . . and more peacemaking . . . the unending
cycle. . . .

in a word . . . I must be saturated with the realization
of your indwelling in me. . . . while I'm being involved
with others. . . .

easy dreams . . . leaving behind what I'm doing
now . . . to go to the poor . . . the culturally
deprived . . . to underdeveloped nations . . . to the
emotionally disturbed . . . educationally robbed . . .
the black ghetto . . . the illiterate . . . I want so much
to be involved . . . meaningfully . . . it's good to dream
in an idealistic and selfless way . . . an emptying
way. . . .

yet how can I be certain . . . that my desire to be
involved . . . is coextensive with your manifest
will? . . . especially when I find it so difficult even to
be courteous . . . to those who can't see it my way? . .
when I won't make the effort to *let* people be
different . . . let alone *help* them to be different? . . .
to aid them or at least allow them . . . to be
themselves? . . .

in the office . . . in the classroom as teacher . . . in
the dorm as student . . . in the factory . . . on top

of a phone pole . . . down in a manhole . . . in
chapel . . . in the rectory . . .in the community
room . . . in the kitchen . . . at a cocktail party . . .
on the football field . . . at a dance . . . wherever
I am . . . whatever I'm doing . . . on a realistic
basis . . . in an immediate way . . . in any simultaneous
moment . . . I must be involved with You . . . and
them . . . precisely because the first *is* first . . . and
the second . . . like unto it. . . .

Love

People are complaining in this age of renewal . . .
God within me . . . that we're letting go of our
principles of morality . . . and all we do is talk about
love. . . .

someone said to me recently . . . "teach those kids
principles . . . all this talk about love . . . pretty soon
there'll be nothing but love" . . . you get the
impression . . . Trinity within us . . . that somehow
these supporters of "sound doctrine" . . . are
propounders of a crossword Gospel . . . and that
love that knows no limit . . . has been reduced to a
numerical morality. . . .

as if Christ had said . . . "by this shall men know you
are my followers . . . that you have an exact account
of the number and kinds of your sins". . . .

or love which must be whole . . . can be shattered
into a schedule-morality . . . fifteen minutes in

thanksgiving after Communion . . . a half hour of
spiritual reading a day . . . confession once a week
or once a month . . . as though love could be
measured . . . by time . . . rather than by intensity . . .
as though the routine becomes the content . . . of
love . . . as though practices are more important than
attitudes. . . .

in either case . . . it seems to be a self-necessitation . . .
which is difficult to relate to the Good News of
love . . . a love that's free . . . spontaneous . . .
numerical and schedule-morality . . . almost seem
to be a worship of Fate . . . leading on the one hand
to the scrupulous cultivation of a guilt complex . . .
or on the other to a legalistic perfectionism. . . .

this is what happens when we drift away . . .
historically . . . from the consciousness of You within
us . . . and develop a spirituality of "things" . . . this
is what occurs when we get all confused . . . about
love and morality . . . when we succumb to the
"Tyranny of the It" (as Roy Rhin puts it) . . . and
define basic Christ-teaching . . . in antiseptic
formulations. . . .

chastity, for example, can become simply "power
to regulate" . . . nothing about interpersonal
responsibilities . . . nothing about behavioral
attitudes . . . just reduce everything to barren
formulas . . . that can be recited. . . .

and confusion can be compounded . . . young men
and women . . . for instance . . . often destroy what
is beautiful between them . . . bound as they are . . .
to the pursuit of the misunderstood . . . smoldering
with resentment . . . or puncturing the sacred . . .
with the needles of flippancy . . . an almost frigid
approach to duty . . . by some religious and priests . . .
even alongside a "deep piety" . . . all in the name of
principles . . . even while mouthing love. . . .

once love is emptied out of morality . . . then the
goodness or evil of an act . . . is measured . . . not
so much by my will's conformity to your will . . .
out of love . . . it depends solely on my action's
conformity to the law . . . legal morality . . . and
within the context of contemporary Christian moral
experience . . . we might question whether such
legal morality is adequate . . . because of the increased
degree of self-consciousness . . . that reveals to
contemporary man his greater ability to be creative . . .
and thus more morally responsible . . . such creative
moral responsibility would be impossible . . . without
the love-context . . . yet there are those . . . who would
take morality out of its context. . . .

before You ever created . . . there was love . . . You,
Father, love your Son . . . and You, Son, return this
love . . . and this love is personified . . . this spirit
of love between You two . . . is a Person . . . You,

51

Spirit of love, are Love itself . . . a limping and
well-worn analogy . . . the love between husband
and wife . . . expressed in the concrete term of a third
person . . . the child. . . .

now when You, God, came to live within me . . .
this eternal activity of love didn't stop . . . St. John
says: "God is love" . . . so You, the immense God . . .
three Persons . . . continue this eternal love affair . . .
among yourselves . . . within *me*. . . .

but more than that . . . You invite me to share in
this exchange of love . . . *and* You expect me to take
the overflow . . . of your love within me . . . and
share it with others . . . boyfriend, girlfriend, husband,
wife, teacher, student, priest, nun, bishop, friend,
enemy, black, white, affluent, indigent . . . people . . .
this is how I can be perfect as You, heavenly Father. . . .

in my love for others . . . I don't have to depend only
on my own impoverished love . . . distorted as it may
be . . . by the grinding complexities of historical
evolution . . . not that I can transcend the history of
warped attitudes about love . . . whether they be
the extravaganzas of situational permissiveness . . .
or the tight-lipped, eye-guarded prissiness of a
disinfected spirituality. . . .

I *can* affirm the meaning of love . . . against all the
distortions that threaten it. . . .

the very love with which we love . . . has been given
to us . . . "the Holy Spirit . . . who has been given to
us . . . has poured God's love into our hearts" . . .
this helps us to escape from a love that is humanly
inauthentic . . . angelized . . . unaffectionate . . . "on
guard" . . . we must avoid the shadow of guilt . . .
that follows a love . . . that is unchristian. . . .

still I'm not just a pipeline for your love . . .
I am a free and active person . . . and You want
my love to be transformed into yours . . . and then
be given to others . . . but it is *my* love that's
being transformed . . . it is with *this* love . . .
divine-human . . . "hypostatic" in action . . . that I
manifest myself . . . as "Christ-I". . . .

if this love of yours . . . generous Three within me . . .
is to be incarnate in me . . . then this means . . . *me* . . .
as human as I am . . . all human . . . and not a
stainless steel version of my humanness . . . especially
with its patronizing contempt of the emotional . . .
against the cardboard background of a canonized
preoccupation . . . with a Jansenistic chastity . . .
which regards everyone as a possible source of
temptation . . . rather than a person to be reached
out to . . . that scrutinizes with stoic detachment . . .
every burst of the emotions . . . to find there the
blossom of another forbidden fruit . . . my love from
myself . . . the authentic me. . . .

sometimes . . . God within us . . . I wonder what
some people mean when they make the Olympian
pronouncement . . . "love means risk" . . . is it some
sort of an aggiornamento "cool" . . . which is nothing
but pure bravado . . . hiding the psychological
regression . . . that's actually taking place? . . .

how can you talk about the "love-risk" . . . and
simultaneously brandish the placard FOR SUBLIMATION
PURPOSES ONLY . . . whenever there is any discussion
on the relevance of the emotions? . . . as though
You gave us our emotional life . . . for no other reason
on earth . . . than to subject it to rational control . . .
negative discipline . . . ruthless adjustment . . . or
even suppression. . . .

"you shall love your neighbor as yourself"? . . .
isn't it slyly ironic . . . that no one questions the
fact . . . that the emotions are essential . . . and must
be cultivated and educated . . . in the thrust of
self-love? . . .

why, then, is emotional expression . . . involvement . . .
suspect . . . when it comes to fleshly . . . social . . .
interpersonal dynamisms? . . . when the "thou" . . .
is introduced? . . .

we may well ponder . . . the revelational validity . . .
of such a pejorative attitude toward the emotions . . .

within the context of Christian love . . . perhaps
we have too theologically adjusted . . . your
communication of love . . . and instead of its breaking
our lives wide open . . . we have succeeded in smashing
it . . . fragmenting it . . . pigeonholing it . . . to fit
every historically accreted compartment . . . since
the Catacomb days . . . and when we're all through . . .
we have a hyper-chastitized . . . nonemotional "thing"
called love . . . while, with all the glandular
enthusiasm we can muster . . . we sing . . . *"God*
is love and he who abides in love . . . abides in God
and God in him". . . .

what is needed is . . . a revamping of attitudes . . .
a realization that love . . . is not a thing . . . but
You! . . . and not You . . . hidden by a mountain of
anthropological relics and customs . . . not You . . .
playing second fiddle . . . to *our* version of your
Word . . . forcing You to try harder . . . because
You're "No. 2" . . . but You inhabiting . . . the
innermost recesses . . . of our being . . . yet remaining
"Other". . . .

perhaps we should restudy . . . Fromm's *The Art
of Loving* . . . then go back and reread . . . the *Song
of Songs* . . . to find out what You within us . . . are
saying to us. . . .

Communication

If I am to become more and more conscious of You within me . . . if I'm going to be more vividly aware . . . I must communicate with You . . . and I mean *communicate* . . . not just "saying prayers" . . . or "getting my prayers in" . . . or "missing my morning prayers" . . . I hate to keep harping . . . Father, Son and Spirit within me . . . but with prayer, too, we seem to be hung up on the same old "I-thing" mentality . . . now it's prayer . . . that's the thing . . . an end in itself . . . an object taken out of real life . . . gingerly placed in some kind of "spiritual baggy" . . . our whole attitude . . . so terribly artificial . . . an acquired posture . . . a narcissistic preoccupation with the way I am "saying" my prayers . . . once again . . . Trinity within me . . . in the very act of being involved with You . . . I am the center. . . .

perhaps . . . for a while at least . . . we should just drop the term "prayer" . . . we must use words that mean something . . . to people . . . in their present

culture . . . even the definition, "a raising of the heart
and mind to God" . . . ephemeral . . . misleading . . .
apersonal . . . systematic . . . classic . . . you sort of
think of taking something . . . out of yourself . . .
then handing it up not even to You . . . but "to
God" . . . lacking that person-to-Person relationship . . .
"to God" . . . what does it mean? . . . how personal
is it? . . . it seems as though . . . I'm like a movie
projectionist . . . I start the thing rolling . . . then
stand back and watch . . . I'm not really in it . . .
I'm not there . . . involved . . . immersed . . . actively
conscious . . . just viewing this heart and mind . . .
being raised "to God". . . .

why not use the word . . . "communication"? . . . it
brings with it . . . a sense of being "there" . . . a
dynamism . . . a realization . . . that You and I are
exchanging . . . it means I must be aware . . . and work
at being aware . . . of You . . . who You are . . . where
You are . . . what You are . . . and of myself . . . when
I believe . . . actively . . . that You are within me . . .
communication is not so difficult . . . it's difficult
only when the one with whom you're trying to
communicate . . . is removed . . . distant . . . foreign . . .
unfamiliar . . . unexperienced . . . a cold concept . . .
then it's tough . . . and sometimes I think . . . this
"raising" . . . pushes You . . . psychologically, at
least . . . away from me . . . makes You sort of a
Wizard of Oz . . . buries you in a cloud . . . that's lost
its symbolism . . . and become the substance called

58

"God" . . . that's when prayer becomes . . . a thing . . .
a thing to be done . . . a thing of obligation . . . a thing
outside myself . . . a thing. . . .

that's when I become preoccupied . . . with form . . .
with words . . . with posture . . . with time . . . with
place . . . with *me* . . . thus, no communication . . . just
"prayer"! . . . what a superficial approach to a great
mystery . . . I am privileged to converse with You . . .
You within me . . . You, concerned and interested. . . .

we can stand on equal footing . . . with You . . .
not groveling . . . not in a position of exaggerated
obeisance . . . this is the privilege: You have dignified
us . . . with your inhabitation . . . made us sharers in
your own nature . . . this is what Grace is all about . . .
and the very fact that You've given us our dignity . . .
keeps us humble . . . as we stand on equal footing
before You . . . we know we don't deserve it . . .
haven't merited it . . . it's not some kind of semipelagian
process . . . by which You find us worthy . . . because
of our good acts . . . and then dignify us . . . with your
inhabitation. . . .

yet . . . we *can* stand before You . . . confident . . .
even bold . . . as equals. . . .

you hear so many . . . complaining that they can't
pray . . . or meditate . . . they've tried . . . but with no
success . . . they've worked on a "composition of

place" . . . on a "nosegay" . . . on a "resolution" . . .
my God within me . . . maybe that's the problem . . .
they're working on a format . . . not on
communication . . . whether we're willing to recognize
it or not . . . the word "prayer" . . . is becoming
obsolete . . . and far worse . . . the mentality and
activity behind the term . . . are fast disappearing . . .
it's the unreality of "praying" . . . that's doing the
damage . . . the stepping out of a real, practical,
familiar, problematic life . . . into an artificial setting . . .
there's overdependence on imagination at the expense
of experience . . . we pose too much . . . assume a
foreign attitude . . . we're not ourselves . . . we strain
to make contact . . . we've got to realize . . . that You
are within us. . . .

we're sincere . . . but that's the tragedy. . . .

we may be saying words . . . and calling them prayer . . .
but am *I* there? . . . do *I* really believe You? . . . in
You? . . . equalizing . . . friendly . . . generous . . .
forgiving . . . personal . . . intimate . . . vitally
interested. . . .

my whole artificial . . . wall-constructing . . . barrier-
erecting approach . . . seems to indicate . . . my refusal
(or inability) to accept You . . . as You've revealed
yourself to me . . . there seems to be some kind of
neurotic consolation . . . in thinking of You as awful . . .

ineffable . . . unapproachable . . . even vengeful . . .
cruel . . . sadistic . . . all-powerful but punitive . . .
omnipresent but snooping . . . forgiving but
tabulating . . . generous but demanding in a selfish
sort of way. . . .

do we really know you? . . . at all? . . .

no wonder we've never *experienced* You . . . *felt* your
presence! . . . no wonder we're satisfied with . . .
"saying our prayers" . . . and getting them in . . .
(really meaning "getting them over with"). . . .

experiencing You . . . disturbs . . . "praying" doesn't . . .
I guess . . . we're just not psychologically present . . .
suppose I'm trying a new recipe . . . or I'm really out
to persuade a customer . . . or I'm going out on a
special date . . . or I'm doing very important research
for a lecture or class . . . or I'm learning my part for
a play . . . or writing a tactful letter . . . or preparing
a sermon for an auspicious occasion . . . then I'm
there! . . . concentrating . . . conscious . . . involved . . .
then there's psychological presence . . . and how! . . .

but when I'm trying to communicate with You? . . .
well, I blame it on distractions . . . what I may be
admitting, however . . . is that I'm putting in too much
time . . . and not enough me . . . and maybe I'm trying
too hard. . . .

if there's something . . . I want . . . desperately . . .
then I'm intense . . . but most of the time . . . there's
that unconscious feeling . . . that You know all
things . . . so why bother telling You . . . what's going
on in my life? . . . my plans . . . my thoughts . . . my
experiences . . . the funny things that happen . . . the
interesting things I've read . . . people I've met . . .
I *will* bring You my problems . . . but so often . . .
that's nothing but the Gigantic-Bayer-Aspirin
approach. . . .

if I could just learn to relax . . . and know You're
within me . . . then . . . when I'm commuting to
work . . . doing the dishes . . . running the sweeper or
dusting . . . running the lawn mower . . . sitting on
the porch or patio . . . having a cup of coffee and a
cigarette . . . (there's a lot of things I do . . .
automatically) . . . then . . . I could be conversing
with You . . . about anything. . . .

let's face it . . . I *do* talk a lot to myself . . . I'm
shaving . . . or getting dressed in the morning . . . and
I'm saying to myself . . . "today I've got to call the
insurance agent . . . get to the bank . . . wash the
children's playclothes . . . answer that letter . . . ask her
for a date . . . take the car in for a checkup . . . go to
the grocery store . . . give that test . . . interview that
salesman . . . cut that class" . . . why can't I address

these me-to-me conversations . . . that go on all day
long . . . to *You* . . . within me? . . .

and if I do begin to converse with You . . . on easy
terms . . . can I, say . . . chat with You about things? . . .
talk things over? . . . share? . . . and why can't I . . . if
I'm really communicating? . . . anyway . . . why don't
I use . . . real language? . . . it's just another sign of
artificiality . . . the way I change to pompous,
organ-sounding verbiage . . . interspersed with the
staccato notes . . . of "thees" . . . "thous" . . .
"shouldsts" . . . "wouldsts" . . . "vouchsafes" . . . why
don't I talk with You . . . God intimately within me . . .
as I do with any close friend? . . . in normal, everyday
language. . . .

to become familiar . . . we must *be* familiar . . . if I
can't open up to You within me . . . I'll never open
up . . . to others. . . .

Trinity within me . . . it's dawning on me! . . . *what*
is the big fuss about "prayer"? . . . here I go again! . . .
we've compartmentalized it . . . that's what . . . "prayer
life," as it's called . . . has been like entering into a
respectable vacuum . . . with "God" . . . the
indwelling . . . presented (when it was) . . . as so
tremendous . . . forbidding . . . that you were made to
think . . . you had to wait . . . for your first levitation . . .
that you had to be well into the so-called Unitive

Way . . . before you could even dare contemplate the fact . . . that the Trinity inhabited you . . . it was an end-of-the-narrow-road reward . . . it's been a lamentable betrayal . . . of the rigid ascetical divisions . . . consecrated by unscrutinized custom . . . we do complicate matters. . . .

You are within me . . . instead of talking to myself . . . I talk to You. . . .

we are what we think . . . and we'll think . . . partially at least . . . what we "pray" . . . and if we grow more conscious of You . . . within us . . . through genuine and dynamic conversation . . . then we'll begin to think . . . in a God-communication atmosphere . . . and your presence will flood us . . . with consciousness. . . .

Worship

There is a concern . . . a worry . . . Trinity within
me . . . that perhaps the stress on community . . . will
have the effect of turning the Christian life . . . into a
very outward thing . . . maybe there won't be any
room for prayer . . . or reflection . . . or interior life . . .
or even thought. . . .

this could possibly happen . . . if "community" is
understood only in terms of people to be *served* . . .
without recognizing people to be *formed*. . . .

again the need for equal emphasis. . . .

extreme outwardness could occur . . . being doers
without the Word . . . as a reaction against
"community" . . . viewed as people bound together
by juridical bonds only . . . with no reference to
sacramental unity . . . against "community" as a rigid
moralistic construction . . . a reaction characterized by

a hyperactivity devoted to "saving" those . . . who have been poured . . . ambiguously . . . into an amorphous blob . . . called "community" . . . a reaction that has now made some feel like . . . uncomfortable fugitives . . . seeking a balance . . . a perspective . . . they accept neither the "heresy of good works" . . . nor the schism of a prayerless religion. . . .

where do we start . . . Father, Son, Spirit . . . indwelling? . . .

the paradox is that we've been lumped together . . . and called "community" . . . but when we *come* together . . . to worship . . . we are isolationists . . . frigid . . . self-conscious . . . it seems that what we want is to be . . . individuals . . . with personal worth . . . willingly formed into the community . . . and not just spectators at an orgy of bedazzling rubrics . . . apparently accomplishing the incidental. . . .

liturgical reform . . . will continue to be superficial . . . extraneous . . . unpenetrating . . . noninvolving . . . until there is a change of attitude . . . until we are no longer satisfied . . . with calling external conformity . . . liturgical reform . . . until we become more conscious . . . (just conscious?) . . . of your inhabitating love . . . in me . . . in her . . . in him . . . in them . . . in us . . . there seems to be some concern, too . . . about young people . . . not too impressed . . . with the

"new" liturgy . . . looking for something else . . . less
fearful of the Sunday mandate . . . of course, if this is
true . . . we can denounce them . . . but not win
them . . . we can castigate . . . but not lead . . . we can,
in some cases, force . . . but not convince . . . maybe
they're exasperated . . . at what Father Gene Kennedy
calls . . . "the false god of physical community" . . .
maybe they want to know . . . why the priest offers
them the chalice . . . "take and drink from this " . . .
while they sing "eat his body, drink his blood" . . .
yet need special permission to do just that . . . good
order, yes . . . but do they see in their uncluttered
incisiveness . . . the contradiction in the arbitrary? . . .
maybe they're starved . . . for an act of worship . . .
that is appropriate for their needs . . . (and why
not?). . . .

we tend to hear our young people . . . but not listen . . .
are we so wise . . . with the wisdom of age . . . that we
can't learn . . . from the fresh insights of youth? . . .

when they do speak out . . . usually with sincerity . . .
we seem almost eager to slam them back . . . into
preconceived categories . . . "rebellious" . . .
"ingrates" . . . "inexperienced" . . . it is possible that
the plush hucksters . . . the soft-selling marketeers . . .
have so twisted and turned young people's heads . . .
from the time they were pre-teens . . . that they don't
know *where* they want to go . . . so they just lash
out. . . .

it is also possible . . . that we can discover from
them . . . a symptom of what is wrong with our
worship . . . after all, young people who go for
anything new and different . . . don't seem too
impressed . . . with changes . . . that adults think are
revolutionary . . . volcanic . . . maybe . . . eternal Three
within . . . I'm oversimplifying . . . by using young
people as an acid test . . . capricious . . . whimsical . . .
changeable . . . uncertain . . . yet they are intense . . .
generous . . . incisive . . . no-nonsense observers . . . of
the current scene . . . of the world . . . they must
redeem . . . I don't think we can dismiss them . . . nor
call their criticisms . . . immature and shallow. . . .

if You, Spirit . . . speak *to* the Church . . . as well as
through it . . . then, perhaps, your handiest megaphone
right now . . . is our youth. . . .

anyway, Trinity within us, what we all need . . .
young . . . middle-aged . . . old . . . is the realization . . .
of your dwelling within us . . . that would have the
impact of duly jarring our theological wisdom
teeth. . . .

just imagine! . . . if we were all growing in the
consciousness . . . of your indwelling . . . each day in
the week . . . not only in myself . . . but in all others . . .
if I were to love You . . . and communicate with You . . .

not only within myself . . . but in all others . . . if I were to treat myself . . . act toward others . . . in the conscious faith . . . that we are your dwelling places . . . just imagine what would happen . . . when we gathered around the Table . . . to be formed into community. . . .

I think we're all admitting . . . the unsatisfactory experience . . . of worshipping . . . a distant God . . . vague . . . aloof . . . a word . . . we know You are "Other" . . . but we haven't grasped the fact that . . . You are "Other" . . . within us . . . I can envision a tremendous act of worship! . . . all of us gathered in the consciousness of your dwelling within us . . . community springing from within . . . and not a superimposed veneer . . . what a basis of formation! . . . what a motive for service! . . .

it just may be that we've been starting at the wrong place . . . in liturgical reform . . . and it's not enough . . . just to give homilies . . . on your indwelling . . . the entire liturgical act could be geared . . . to fostering this awareness . . . our Mass prayers so often give the impression . . . of an imperialist "Lord" . . . couldn't they be reformed . . . to bring out this basic belief . . . You dwell within us . . . loving . . . friendly . . . equalizing . . . intimate? . . . would it be so radical . . . to ask that a prayer begin "O God within us" . . . instead of the stern and

faraway "O God" . . . or "through Jesus Christ, your
Son, our Brother, who lives with You and the Holy
Spirit in us . . . now and forever" . . . or "loving
Trinity, dwelling within us . . . we come to this altar
to offer Jesus Christ, our victim, whom You have
identified us with"? . . . the riches are too plentiful . . .
to be sacrificed for the sake of a spartan . . .
emotionless . . . clipped . . . speedy . . . non-
thought-provoking format . . . who says the Western
mind likes this? . . .

either we believe . . . and act out our belief . . . or we're
just mouthing . . . we've got to get away . . . from that
metaphysical mentality . . . that reserves your
indwelling for mystics . . . it's for all! . . . we've got to
stop . . . making arbitrary qualifications . . . more
essential than essential beliefs . . . must order . . . to
be preserved . . . reach into every crevice? . . .

the basic . . . the overwhelming essential is . . . that we
are able to *worship* . . . precisely because You do dwell
within us . . . Father . . . Son . . . Spirit . . . immense . . .
eternal . . . all powerful . . . God . . . *within us!* . . . if
we would absorb this fact . . . then liturgical details . . .
all details for that matter . . . would be seen in
perspective . . . and nonessentials would be adapted . . .
or discarded . . . and quickly . . . so that the needs of
the community would be served . . . more
relevantly . . . insuring its formation . . . more
continuously. . . .

the fundamental value . . . is You within us . . . within
me . . . there are other values . . . valid because of
historical circumstances . . . and as history evolves . . .
their validity ceases . . . if we would live in the
consciousness of your indwelling . . . then we wouldn't
be bogged down . . . with rigid statements of
obligations and prohibitions . . . about invalid
values . . . and we would not be frightened into
immobility . . . by a detailed tariff of penalties for
transgressions . . . reducing good order . . . to the
level of mere propriety. . . .

and all the while, You . . . Trinity . . . want us to be
relaxed . . . friendly . . . loving . . . comfortable . . .
so much so . . . that You Three have come . . . to make
your home within us. . . .

Eternal Three within me . . . your saving act is to
rescue us . . . from impersonalism . . . this is your
will . . . it must be ours . . . we must be patient . . .
because we're human . . . and we know You write
straight with crooked lines . . . yet when it comes to
worshipping You . . . perhaps the reaction of our
youth today . . . is your shorthand . . . can we be so
patient . . . as not to transcribe? . . .

Christ-I

Certainly, Trinity within us . . . one of the most
insidious problems of our times . . . one whose
handwriting is still fresh on the wall of modern
social malaise . . . is impersonalism . . . students
complaining . . . bitterly but by no means
inarticulately . . . about being IBM cards . . . workers
in industry . . . feeling "punched-out" at the very
moment when they punch in . . . just a number . . .
"rapidation" . . . has done a lot of this . . . so has
assembly-line government . . . so has the
"you-can't-really-win-you-can't-really-lose" kind
of suspended social animation . . . we tend to see
people with dull-eyed custom . . . poor . . . culturally
deprived . . . Negro . . . underachiever . . . affluent . . .
illiterate . . . conservative . . . liberal . . . reactionary . . .
and once we categorize anyone . . . then this concrete,
human being . . . this precious person . . . fades
anonymously into his roped-off section of the faceless
masses . . . even beyond troubling statistics. . . .

houses peopled with husbands . . . disgruntled at
being such easily replaced cogs . . . wives resentful
at being "grass widows" . . . because their husbands
are so taken with their mistresses . . . called "job" . . .
teen-agers whose lives grumble eloquently against
the tidy moral universe . . . of their elders . . . old
folk who feed on the lonely memories . . . of the days
before Affluentia. . . .

there's a lot of talk today . . . eternal Three within . . .
about identity crises . . . talk that shouldn't be too
casually sloughed off . . . it's talk that has about it a
sort of freakish eloquence. . . .

today's person . . . experiences the inability . . . to feel
his own identity . . . he *feels* impersonal . . . he recoils
from a world . . . whose masochistic cult . . . pontificates
in a social vacuum . . . exercising power and not
explaining it . . . he recoils from an impersonal
world . . . frightened back into himself . . . only to
find there a stranger . . . he is alone . . . and he feels
his loneliness . . . he doesn't feel loved . . . and that,
God within us . . . is *the* crime of our era . . . today's
person . . . is all of us. . . .

sometimes . . . Father, Son and Spirit . . . within all
of us . . . we turn to religion . . . yet here, too, we feel
perhaps abandoned . . . by hairsplitting officials . . .
or perhaps unled . . . by either smooth-tongued or

quite undiplomatic leaders . . . (even those on the
lowest rung) . . . we feel this way at least from time
to time . . . all the while . . . we're looking for
someone . . . who will tell us . . . You are not
distant . . . not an abstract God . . . that You have not
become impersonal. . . .

I wonder how many of us . . . have ever *really*
experienced . . . the joy and the torment of love . . .
in our relationship with You! . . .

we want to be shown . . . how we can find our
identity . . . our personableness . . . our reality. . . .

it's not so much that You are dead . . . as it is that our
love . . . has never really been alive! . . .

while we're looking . . . You are within us . . . out of
love . . . You have made your intimate invasion . . .
into our innermost beings. . . .

all of us . . . loving Three within us . . . are growing
tired, it seems . . . of lazy answers, retread responses
and sedative solutions . . . we want it to be real . . . yet
your indwelling . . . so fundamental . . . so real . . .
so basic . . . is still a theological weak sister . . . looked
upon with scientific detachment by so many. . . .

we are evolving in Salvation History . . . yes . . . but
in Perdition History, too . . . a context of brutish

depravity . . . cowardice . . . greed . . . hypocrisy . . .
violence . . . from which we desire salvation . . . yet,
so often, our questions are equated . . . with tinkering
with the bureaucratic machinery . . . while we are
proffered periodic doses . . . of what Martin Luther
King called . . . "pious irrelevancies and sanctimonious
trivialities" . . . occasionally dashed with platitudes . . .
and they're offered . . . almost as a catalytic check . . .
on total despair . . . as a panacea . . . for our corrosively
negative impersonalism. . . .

yet . . . through your action . . . called baptism . . . Christ
Jesus . . . You have brought about . . . mysteriously
and "significantly" . . . an incorporation . . . a real
identity . . . between yourself and us . . . each of us . . .
retains his own unique identity . . . while I take on
your identity and You take on mine . . . mystery . . .
inspiring not awe and wonder . . . but simply
mystery . . . that registers a little above zero . . . on
the credibility scales . . . an "object" of belief . . . and
while we're searching . . . almost violently . . . for
religious relevancy for ourselves and others . . . a fact
of imperative priority . . . lies unobserved in full
view . . . and available to *all* of us . . . not just
mystics! . . .

in your eyes . . . Father within me . . . a new individual
emerges . . . who is each of us . . . Christ and I . . . I
really become You, Christ . . . so that I can say . . .
"I am Christ" . . . without absorbing your identity . . .

so that You lose it . . . and without losing my own . . .
"I live, no not I, but Christ lives in me" . . . and You,
Christ, truly become me . . . without ceasing to be
yourself . . . and I become You . . . without ceasing to
be me . . . and so, Father . . . in your eyes . . . there's a
new individual whose name is . . . "Christ-I". . . .

my God within me! . . . I've got to believe this! . . .
my name is "Christ-I" . . . what a need for a dynamic
faith! . . . to be consciously aware . . . of my identity . . .
warm . . . *personal* . . . who am I? . . . I am Christ-I . . .
this is what your living Word has taught us, Father . . .
this is the Light You bring us, Spirit . . . and we must
accept or be judged . . . (for mystics only?) . . . "every
man who rejects me . . . and will not accept my
sayings . . . has a judge . . . the very words I have
spoken" . . . for so long . . . we have heard your
words . . . Christ Jesus . . . but have we believed
them? . . . I mean . . . *really* believed . . . or have
your words become so familiar . . . that they have no
impact? . . . will it be said of us . . . as it was said of
the Israelites in the desert . . . "yet the message
proclaimed to them . . . did them no good . . . because
they only heard . . . and did not believe as well"? . . .
(St. Paul). . . .

I am Christ-I . . . I have an identity . . . it is personal . . .
to the point of mystery. . . .

we must maintain equal emphasis . . . on the terms of

this identification . . . Christ-I . . . yet in this psychodynamic age . . . of vigorous or pathological self-consciousness . . . what consciousness should I be perceiving? . . . I am real . . . and You, Christ, are real . . . now, *how* real? . . . where real? . . . the forces of impersonalism . . . in this day and age . . . are formidable . . . how shall I glory in my weaknesses? . . .

You proposed the prototype of this identity . . . Christ . . . "I ask," You said . . . "that they all may be one . . . as You, Father, are in me . . . and I in You . . . they may also be one in us . . . I in them and You in me". . . .

it's as though You are saying to me . . . (in the continuous now) . . . "give me your hands . . . your feet . . . your mind . . . your lips . . . your eyes . . . your ears . . . your emotions . . . your affective life . . . your whole being . . . that I may continue . . . now . . . here on earth . . . to love our Father . . . to save our brothers and sisters . . . in and through you". . . .

if I had the faith! . . . I could rid my life once and for all . . . of the inertia . . . born of impersonalism . . . the manikin-like practice of religion . . . but I've got to believe! . . . I've got to not only know my own identity . . . Christ-I . . . but I must identify myself . . . to and for others. . . .

by myself . . . I can't do much . . . to clear the psychic

smog . . . of impersonalism . . . if many of us . . .
could become . . . convinced? . . . fascinated? . . .
obsessed? . . . with our identity . . . the total impact . . .
on our society . . . could be the most compassionate
reform . . . of history . . . just overwhelming. . . .

what is needed . . . is a defiant revival of belief . . . in
your sayings . . . Christ Jesus . . . an almost orgiastic
enthusiasm . . . that will smash into insignificant
pieces . . . that boxed-in propriety . . . which is
seemingly always assumed to be . . . "holiness" . . .
which isolates . . . which contributes . . . like a
cancer . . . to the impersonalism . . . that causes us
to feel unloved. . . .

Christ-We

So much is starting to fall into place . . . Trinity within
me . . . I think this happens when you have a central
truth . . . that's really essential . . . that's more an
experienced atmosphere . . . than merely a textbook
truth . . . or even an assimilated, although still
very objective, truth . . . impersonalism . . . even if it
is interwoven in our social fabric . . . doesn't seem to
be the threat I once thought it was . . . I'm pondering
more my identity . . . consciously. . . .

yet I do realize that if I'm satisfied with just that . . .
I could well be an isolationist . . . as impersonal as I
claim society is . . . selfish . . . regarding my
identity . . . as Christ-I . . . as a buried treasure . . .
or worse . . . as a reason for snobbery . . . lording it
over those who are still alone . . . isolated . . .
unloved . . . still pierced by impersonalism. . . .

equal emphasis . . . demands not only my
enlightenment . . . but that of others, too . . . after

all the insight is not mine . . . miserly . . . due to me
and my cleverness . . . Titus was reminded: "when
the kindness of God our savior and his love toward
men appeared . . . he saved us in his mercy . . . not by
virtue of any moral achievement of ours . . . but by
the moral renewal of the Holy Spirit". . . .

as I said . . . Father . . . Son . . . Spirit . . . within me . . .
loving me . . . giving me identity . . . I must identify
myself . . . to and for others. . . .

if I don't . . . I'll soon find that knowing my own
identity . . . isn't enough . . . I still hunger to relate . . .
meaningfully . . . to others . . . in fact, if I don't relate,
I'll never become dynamically aware . . . of my
identity. . . .

it's just not enough to know that *I* am Christ-I . . .
I must seek out . . . and relate . . . to this person whose
name is Christ-I . . . that person . . . who is Christ-I . . .
to the community who is Christ-we! . . .

if your saving love . . . Trinity inhabiting me . . . is to
rescue us . . . from impersonalism . . . then I who
share in your saving love . . . who am having my love
transformed into yours . . . then I must contribute
whatever I can . . . to the total impact . . . of this, our
love . . . upon the worldwide condition . . . of
impersonalism . . . as we search the outer reaches of

space . . . our planet seems to be shrinking . . . to
atom size . . . psychologically, we've grown used
to worldwide movements . . . and events . . .
Communism . . . the United Nations . . . the other
side of the globe flashes instantaneously on our TV
screens. . . .

I can't afford . . . to shy away from involvement in
the needs of others . . . to submit to an age of such
narrow purviews . . . Christianity . . . God within . . .
will never succeed with total impact . . . until Christ-we
are as concerned with the person nearest . . . and the
one farthest away . . . and the stranger right next to
us . . . and not just fascinated either . . . I can't
afford . . . to sink imperceptibly . . . into the anonymous
masses . . . even worse . . . to live out a smug,
ritualistic spirituality . . . by rote. . . .

if I do . . . I'll eventually lose my identity . . . become
impersonal . . . I can't afford this impoverishing
spiritual affluence. . . .

besides identifying myself . . . to others . . . I must
search for ways . . . to help others . . . to reveal their
identity to me . . . to do this . . . I must be as conscious
of your identification with them . . . as I am of yours
with me . . . it's rather a simple . . . habituated life . . .
that takes care of all obligations . . . keeps the rules . . .
"does good" . . . You know . . . get it out of the

way . . . so I can get back to me . . . isolated and impersonal . . . and consciously unidentified . . . being aware . . . of Christ-them is a full-life challenge . . . tirelessly . . . relentlessly . . . constantly inconvenienced. . . .

Trinity within us . . . deliver us from even allowing . . . our identity . . . to be forged into infinitely codified lives. . . .

when I meet someone . . . I should think atmospherically . . . this person . . . for me . . . in this unrepeatable moment . . . is Christ! . . . "who are you?" . . . "I am Christ-I" . . . "then you are Christ, too!". . .

You said to Paul . . . "I am Jesus whom you are persecuting" . . . so You say to me . . . I am Jesus whom you are meeting . . . with whom you are shaking hands . . . to whom you're giving this quarter . . . whom you are teaching . . . whom you're playing ball with . . . with whom you're sitting in class . . . I am Jesus . . . whose authority you respect . . . whose talent you admit . . . to whom your marital love draws you . . . whom you can't stand . . . whom you emulate . . . whom you correct . . . whom you counsel . . . whom you employ. . . .

what a tremendous mystery of identity! . . . I am

Christ . . . this person is for me Christ . . . someone
has said . . . that Christian living is a search . . . not
an arrival . . . could it be a search for identity? . . .
mine . . . yours . . . his . . . hers . . . theirs . . .
ours? . . .

once I am thoroughly convinced . . . of the Christ-I . . .
Christ-they identity . . . once this mystery has become
part and parcel . . . of my very lifeblood . . . once it
is an automatic reflex mentality . . . once it is the
atmosphere . . . in which I live, breathe and have my
being . . . then . . . God within me . . . I don't stop . . .
pleased to the point of delirium . . . this is the
psychological . . . now it's time to act . . . I move . . .
reach out to . . . this concrete . . . perhaps pitiable . . .
always precious . . . living, breathing human being . . .
to this friendly . . . or disagreeable . . . thoughtful . . .
or demanding . . . meek . . . or haughty . . . real,
flesh-and-blood person. . . .

as I said about my own identity . . . although You,
Christ . . . do in some mysterious way . . . identify
with me . . . I do *not* lose my own unique identity . . .
I remain "Christ-I" . . . and I must maintain equal
emphasis on both terms of the identification . . . so,
too, this person . . . with whom You've also
identified . . . remains uniquely himself . . . and I
cannot say I love You . . . Christ . . . in him . . .
without loving him himself. . . .

85

"if anyone says . . . 'I love God' and hates his neighbor . . . he is a liar!" . . . I must relate to this person . . . to these people . . . or else I'll just be fostering a pseudopersonalism . . . to replace the impersonalism . . . that I want desperately to be freed from . . . I'll only be furthering . . . the already tragic travesty . . . of a Christ-identification . . . based on a narcissistic spirituality. . . .

I really don't understand . . . Three loving me within . . . how this mystery of identity works . . . faith is not all illumination . . . there's no strict chronological order . . . "first I see Christ . . . then the person" . . . or "first I meet the person . . . and then remember that Christ has identified with him" . . . sounds like compartments? . . . it's atmosphere . . . I ponder this mystery . . . in my communication with You Three within . . . then sometimes it pops into mind . . . when I meet someone . . . casually . . . formally . . . for the first time . . . or the nth time . . . and most of the time I just don't advert at all . . . but it's there . . . like atmosphere . . . a context . . . I know that when I'm with people . . . I encounter the hard reality of this individual person . . . and the mysterious reality of You . . . Jesus Christ . . . if I don't explicitly remember . . . this mystery . . . or if I'm so taken with the concrete individual . . . that the thought that he is identified with You . . . is unconsciously missing . . .

no need for high-voltage scrupulosity . . . or a savage case of psychological bends. . . .

when two people encounter each other . . . smoothly or clashingly . . . and set up some sort of a relationship . . . it is through this very relationship . . . that the evidence of your identification . . . is either produced or illumined . . . as a bond or a challenge . . . it doesn't matter whether or not . . . I consciously and explicitly say to myself "this person is Christ for me" . . . as long as I don't reflect him away from myself . . . your identification . . . should be unhysterically memorable . . . I must look openly . . . at people. . . .

yet . . . how easy . . . even comforting . . . to go slam-banging past this person . . . all the more if unattractive . . . detestable . . . apparently worthless . . . lazy . . . uncooperative . . . rebellious . . . envious . . . opinionated . . . disobedient . . . doctrinaire . . . poor . . . vulgar . . . dirty . . . self-righteous . . . unsophisticated . . . how easy . . . reassuring . . . "meritorious"? . . . to ignore this awfully . . . disturbingly real person . . . and to love a comfortably unseen Christ . . . an undemanding Christ . . . something like we do with You in your eucharistic presence . . . there You don't bother us . . . so in our neighbor-devotion we don't want to be disturbed either. . . .

when we kneel before You . . . in the Eucharist . . .
we are saying in effect that this same reverence . . .
must be given . . . as a consequence and inevitability . . .
to the next person we meet . . . to all people. . . .

my communication with You . . . stimulates this
awareness . . . You . . . Christ . . . are my identity
crisis. . . .

Christ-They

It is a beautiful theory . . . eternal Three within us . . .
seeking . . . finding . . . loving . . . serving You,
Christ . . . in others . . . but that beauty begins to
become twisted . . . disfigured . . . when it's exposed
to the heat . . . of the blast furnace . . . of hatred . . .
bigotry . . . misunderstanding. . . .

it's a lot easier . . . to issue antiseptic directives . . .
from a safe distance. . . .

I can insulate myself . . . against the hunger . . .
poverty . . . inadequate housing . . . backward
education . . . chronic unemployment . . . outmoded
job training . . . I can insulate myself . . . against
crime . . . violence . . . civil disorder . . . unsatisfactory
medical care . . . antiquated public transportation . . .
insufficient consumer protection . . . tax squeeze for
"defense" . . . inflation . . . gold loss . . . at times . . .
at most times . . . these problems aren't even real to
me . . . I can insulate myself . . . and still seek

"Christ-them" . . . without being truly human . . .
and becoming vulnerable . . . without anguish. . . .

perhaps . . . Trinity within and watching . . . our
theology is not . . . "political" . . . in J. B. Metz's sense
of the term . . . because . . . we are constantly
answering questions . . . not even raised! . . .
because . . . we are habitually knocking down . . .
straw men . . . precariously positioned . . . because . . .
we are frantically busy . . . inbreeding . . .
"tabernacling" our faith . . . giving our tenets of
belief . . . sanctuary . . . politely . . . diplomatically . . .
withdrawing from the public forum. . . .

(a priest faces the stressful and challenging task . . . of
meeting the Negro . . . on his home ground . . .
demonstrating with him . . . fighting side by side . . .
sweating the hot summer . . . as it edges into riots . . .
and is reprimanded . . . for going into bars. . . .)

even when we give notional assent . . . Christ Jesus . . .
to your identification . . . "whatsoever you do to one of
these" . . . we in this concrete day . . . month . . .
year . . . will find some excuse . . . for signing that
petition . . . to keep a Negro family . . . out of our
neighborhood . . . while we "notionally" advocate . . .
human dignity . . . and rights . . . we look at white
"marchers" . . . as being sort of "kooks" . . . or if
we . . . whose name is "Christ-we" . . . hear of

91

some . . . who move into the ghetto . . . to help by
presence . . . as well as words . . . we . . . "Christ-we" . . .
seem to smirk . . . "fadists" . . . and all the while . . .
we plead our . . . "Lord, hear our prayer" . . . in
response to the petition of the Prayer of the
Faithful . . . "that the poor and Negro may be treated
with dignity" . . . of course . . . in a modern . . .
middle-class . . . white . . . parish church . . .
(uninfested with rats). . . .

it's rather simple to *pray* . . . for "Christ-them" . . .
in the ghetto . . . in the alleys . . . in the doorways . . .
in the emergency wards . . . in the brothels . . . in the
trash cans . . . "this Blood . . . is to be shed . . . for
you . . . and for *all* men" . . . how much . . . have I
shed? . . . You . . . who have identified with me? . . .

we'll be very socially concerned . . . as long as You . . .
Christ . . . don't disturb . . . bother . . . challenge us . . .
if You do . . . we just may have to crucify You . . .
again . . . with the more modernized . . . subtle . . .
crucifixion . . . of merely ignoring . . . You-in-them. . . .

of course . . . there are those . . . who *are* socially
concerned . . . vitally . . . vibrantly . . . an almost
incautious enthusiasm . . . marks their desire . . .
to relate meaningfully . . . to others . . . they've had
it . . . with indifference . . . they're tired of
discussing . . . they want to *do* . . . even at great

personal inconvenience . . . even in opposition to
the accepted norms. . . .

from a group of young college students . . . who spend
their Easter vacation working in Appalachia . . . to
perhaps the hippies . . . priests who go into the
ghetto . . . to offer Mass . . . in order to form the
Community . . . in a four-room house . . . home of
three families . . . the Sister dissatisfied with merely
failing a student . . . who seeks him out at home . . .
after hours . . . the family of seven . . . who on
Thanksgiving Day . . . prepare a turkey dinner . . .
only to eat hot dogs and beans . . . then take the
dinner to the "Ward" . . . and give it to a family . . .
whose subsistence all year . . . is hot dogs and beans . . .
these . . . and many . . . want to be involved . . .
personally . . . immediately . . . intimately . . .
concretely. . . .

yet . . . sadly . . . some of these . . . while zestfully
plunging into interpersonal relationships . . . while
zealously rolling up their sleeves . . . while eagerly
scanning the horizons . . . plotting courses into the
unknown . . . straining at the bit . . . some . . . are
totally oblivious . . . of their unchristian response . . .
to the "uninvolved" . . . the comfortable . . . the
reactionary . . . the unadaptable . . . the bigot . . . the
"closed-minded conservatives" . . . as they are
called. . . .

and while they go out to demonstrate . . . or carry
placards . . . or peacefully protest . . . or withdraw
from society . . . or seek responsibility on campus . . .
or update their Order's structure . . . or dialogue
with the bishop on authority . . . or enter discussion
groups with their pastors . . . or instruct a class on
the web of legalism. . . .

perhaps . . . with their frenzy of "involvement" . . .
they will not even be civil . . . or mannerly . . .
or practice the common amenities . . . toward those
with whom they live! . . . why is it . . . for
example . . . that some priests . . . and sisters . . .
and laymen . . . who offer constructive criticism to
"the establishment" . . . to the hierarchy . . . the local
ordinary . . . the pastor . . . the provincial . . . the
superior . . . because of their lack of willingness . . .
to communicate . . . or to be open to ideas other
than their own . . . or to listen . . . or to ask for
advice . . . why is it . . . that these same constructive
critics . . . will resent . . . insult . . . castigate . . .
those who offer constructive criticism of their views
on . . . or version of . . . the aggiornamento? . . .

perhaps . . . the love that they lavish . . . on the
poor . . . the Negro . . . the social outcast . . . the
downtrodden . . . the drunk . . . the prostitute . . .
the unwed mother . . . the prisoner . . . is absent in

their dealings with those . . . who don't see eye-to-eye
with them . . . who hold back . . . who violently
react . . . who disagree . . . there is little or no love . . .
for the "opposition" . . . because they disturb . . .
the "involved" Christian's convictions. . . .

yet . . . are these not also . . . "Christ-they"? . . .
have You . . . Christ Jesus . . . not also identified . . .
with the opponents of involvement . . . or renewal . . .
or social concern . . . or updating . . . as much as
You have . . . with the poor . . . the ghetto-dweller . . .
the abandoned? . . .

a shocking twist . . . in the bizarre debate . . .
between the "liberals" and "conservatives" . . . is
the inescapable fact that . . . some liberals who go
around preaching freedom . . . will deny the
conservatives . . . the freedom to disagree! . . . is a
closed-minded liberal . . . any more Christian . . .
than a closed-minded conservative? . . . if the
distinction is valid . . . that the conservative is
characterized by devotion . . . to the "institution" . . .
and the liberal . . . by devotion . . . to the "person" . . .
then the liberal should be much more sympathetic
and understanding . . . of an opposing point of
view . . . yet one of the most intriguing psychological
developments . . . in this age of renewal . . . seems to
be the fact . . . that the liberal is very open-minded . . .
until he meets someone . . . who disagrees with

him . . . he can even retaliate with harshness . . .
be vindictive toward . . . the very *person* . . . he
should be favoring. . . .

Trinity within us . . . those who espouse
involvement . . . with Christ-them . . . must
understand . . . that not all the poor . . . live in
hovels . . . there are those who suffer . . . from poverty
of relevance . . . from poverty of courage to
change . . . from poverty of vision . . . from poverty
of the understanding . . . of the meaning of "political"
theology . . . we must relate to them, too . . . the
darkness of skin . . . is not the only line . . . of
segregation . . . there is the darkness of fear . . .
the darkness of withdrawal . . . the darkness of
inability to relate meaningfully . . . they, too,
are Christ-they . . . disturbingly demanding
our love . . . our relationship . . . our compassion . . .
in fact . . . from a "liberal" point of view . . . perhaps
these "poor" . . . these "colored" . . . more than any
others . . . are the "least of my brethren" . . . whom
we must treat . . . as we would treat You . . . Christ. . . .

in both instances . . . the so-called conservative . . .
and liberal . . . what is needed . . . is the burning
realization . . . of our mutual identity . . . because of
your incessant activity within us . . . Father, Son,
Spirit . . . a realization that can merge . . . the
differing centers of interest . . . that can smoothe
the way . . . to frank and genuinely loving . . .

intercommunication . . . without fear of reprisal . . .
or caustic barbs . . . without ruthlessly demolishing . . .
points that were never made . . . so that we can all
become . . . aware in faith . . . that Christ-I . . . and
Christ-they . . . are really . . . Christ-we . . . and that
our relating to one another . . . is based . . . on a
pre-established unity . . . thanks to You . . . Three
within us . . . through You, Christ . . . our Identifier. . . .

The Numbness of Rash Judgment

We cannot be insensitively numb . . . divine Three
within us . . . toward this concrete human being . . .
as he is in himself . . . if we are to be honest in
seeking You out . . . Christ . . . in him . . . identified
with him . . . the thrust of your basic ethic . . . is
to love one another with the kind of love . . . You
have for each of us . . . because we'll be judged
with the very same kind of judgment . . . this is why
your relationship . . . with the currently righteous . . .
was one of excoriating their condemnatory judgments
of others . . . what seems to kick the ladder . . .
from beneath your ideal . . . then . . . is rash
judgment. . . .

no evidence . . . suspicion . . . fictionalizing . . . a bit
of truth, some secondhand stories and a lot of gossip
. . . faultfinding . . . circumstantial possibilities . . .
peering into motives . . . the arched brow of
omniscience . . . the smile of condescending
patience . . . everything . . . that invades . . .

injures . . . cripples . . . destroys . . . my God within
me . . . rash judgment! . . . and worst of all . . . this,
in your name . . . Christ . . . all this . . . cloaked in
the garments of righteousness . . . "for their own
good" . . . "for the good of 'the Church' " . . . all
in the name of "fraternal correction" . . . how many
have been reduced to subhuman self-appraisal? . . .
made moral vegetables? . . . how many have had their
hearts . . . torn right out? . . . how many . . . totally
defenseless . . . have been destroyed? . . . utterly . . .
driven to drink? . . . out of the Church? . . . away
from You, Christ? . . . into total despair? . . . the
existential emptiness of being unwilling . . . then
unable to trust . . . confidences . . . sold to any
bidder . . . betrayed . . . the bitterness and cynicism
fallout . . . from the loss of faith . . . in one's
fellowman. . . .

and all the while . . . Father, Son and Spirit . . . You
watch us . . . from within . . . attacking "other
Christs" . . . robbing them . . . throwing them on
the roadside . . . leaving them to die. . . .

"Bless me, Father, I have sinned . . . and I was
uncharitable a few times". . . .

uncharitable? . . . I'm being forgiven a sin . . . I don't
even understand! . . . I really don't know what I do . . .
the extent of the damage . . . I can demolish . . .
another human being . . . precious . . . sacred . . .

100

identified! . . . ruthlessly judge . . . heartlessly turn
off . . . brutally condemn . . . righteously report to
the "proper authorities" . . . mercilessly harass . . .
confidentially spread "what I've heard" . . . and
then? . . . and then off to another tongue-thrusting
trip . . . to the table of the Lord . . . to eat the Bread . . .
that we "all may be one". . . .

you can say all you want . . . about the "human
condition" . . . but this is inhuman! . . . the sin? . . .
casual inhumanity. . . .

vultures . . . we feed on your Body . . . Christ Jesus . . .
leave . . . and feed on one another . . . a perversion! . . .
and all in the name of religion . . . all under the title
"Christian"! . . .

"Bless me, Father . . . and I gossiped a bit". . . .

and another human being . . . ideals shattered . . .
courage drained . . . eyes tearless for the lack of
any more tears . . . a heart shriveled . . . trust
evaporated . . . the vacuum of no one to go to . . . the
living suicide of meaninglessness . . . disillusionment . . .
despondency . . . disenchantment . . . isolation . . .
alienation . . . loneliness . . . person-ache . . . going
through the motions of living . . . a wasteland of
emotional coexistence . . . despair . . . where once
enthusiasm flourished . . . agony . . . where once
forward-looking joy . . . spilled over from a heart . . .

full of love . . . inertia . . . where once raced the
desire . . . for the martyrdom of good works. . . .

and why? . . . Love within me . . . why? . . . because
of the careless barbarism . . . of the "filler sins". . . .

after all . . . when in doubt . . . pad the list . . . with
a few sins of "uncharitableness" . . . as long as we
fulfill our duties . . . after all, what else are we going
to talk about? . . . as long as my obligations are
taken care of . . . that's what really counts . . . "talking
about people"? . . . just part of living . . . nobody's
perfect . . . you have to have *some* faults! . . . my
prayers are said . . . my soul is clean . . . anyhow . . .
"uncharitableness" is only a venial sin . . . a slight
offense . . . from *my* point of view. . . .

how does it look from yours . . . Trinity within me? . . .

Appearances and Motives

When I judge another . . . without sufficient evidence
to draw a final conclusion . . . yet . . . still draw it . . .
when I know full well . . . that I can't know another
person's motives . . . yet . . . still impute them . . .
then . . . I am basing my judgments on appearances. . .
"I know why he did that" . . . "well if he thinks for
one moment . . . that I'll accept *that* explanation" . . .
"who's *he* trying to kid?" . . . and if I have
prejudged . . . another's motives . . . and if he tells
me what they really were . . . I just don't accept
them . . . "he's covering" . . . "after all, I wasn't
born yesterday!" . . .

yet . . . I know in my own case . . . that any given
motive for any particular action . . . can be modified
or abandoned . . . within the act . . . motives seem to
bristle with complexity . . . I begin donating to the
poor . . . if not extravagantly, at least with an
unobsessive regularity . . . for your honor and glory . . .
and to please You . . . by being fulfilled in a

103

self-emptying generosity . . . and, then, right in
the middle of my gospeled prodigality . . .
imperceptibly . . . somehow self-fulfillment is replaced
with self-gratification . . . I like the praise . . . I want
to be extolled . . . and in our drenched-in-images
society . . . my motive changes . . . fanfare and
confetti . . . how often can we point to a pure
motive . . . for any action? . . . yet . . . I presume that I
can lock my eye . . . onto the keyhole of another's
actions . . . and squint into the deepest recesses . . .
of his heart . . . then call out . . . the dimensional
quality . . . of his motives . . . when, perhaps, he isn't
certain himself . . . what his motives are. . . .

a boy and a girl . . . are seen frequently together . . .
because they have found a healthy relationship? . . .
or because they can easily sin? . . . which motive
do we attribute? . . . do we try to "break them up" . . .
because we're sincerely concerned . . . about the
possibility of sin? . . . or because we've already judged
them as sinning? . . . are we genuinely preoccupied
with the debilitating effect . . . sin has on human
development? . . . or do we experience a kind of
seismic shock of . . . self-satisfying righteousness . . .
judgment as a venture? . . . how many of our
judgments . . . are based on appearances . . . and on
circumstantial evidence? . . . how many of our
judgments are the result of our reluctance . . . to
impute anything but the basest . . . most licentious . . .
selfish . . . manipulating . . . graceless . . . insidious . . .

motives . . . always ulterior! . . . to people's actions . . .
how easy . . . lethal . . . our judgments! . . .

but my prayers are said . . . and my soul is clean. . . .

I say I believe . . . You are indwelling in others . . .
but to adore and love You . . . Father, Son and
Spirit . . . in others . . . is equivalent to admitting that
they are in the state of grace . . . but who can be
certain that another person is in the state of grace? . . .
so . . . rather than presuming goodness . . . and
adoring You . . . in a person . . . that You *might* not
be indwelling . . . with the self-assurance characteristic
of the righteous . . . I opt for your absence . . . and
I don't adore You in others . . . and eventually . . .
the evacuation of all memory . . . of your indwelling
in others . . . and having grown reverently mindless . . .
of this mystery . . . I also forget about your identifying
with others . . . Christ . . . and so this human
being . . . becomes an easier prey . . . for the
cunning . . . incisive . . . intuitive judgments . . . that
are my talent. . . .

and this is how piety . . . becomes a travesty . . .
and this is how some people . . . the more pious they
seem to get . . . the more righteous they seem to
become . . . and the more prone they are . . . to indulge
in lacerating judgments . . . cruelty with a halo? . . .
it is . . . psychologically, at least . . . a Godless piety . . .
a sanctity without You . . . a holiness that is

105

idolatry . . . a morality that is stiff-shirtism . . . thus
the unappeasable itch . . . to judge and condemn
others . . . that I might robe myself in chasubled
exaltation . . . since You are nowhere around . . . in
my holiness . . . to exalt me. . . .

only a venial sin . . . a slight offense. . . .

within the same heart . . . a fervent effort to be
pious . . . and a see-through holiness . . . that must
defensively . . . judge and condemn. . . .

the Pharisee. . . .

a moral dwarf . . . casting a long shadow . . . because
he stands in the light of his neon castigations. . . .

Neo-Pharisaism

In my desire . . . and I hope it's sincere . . . to condemn
self-righteousness in others . . . in excoriating
pharisaism . . . in order to nudge consciences . . .
I myself must be most careful . . . not to become
self-righteous . . . not to perch on the end . . . of the
legalistic limb . . . I'm trying to saw off . . . not to
assume the mantle of . . . a neo-Pharisee . . . this can
happen . . . quite easily . . . glibly . . . I identify with
the Prodigal . . . the Magdalene . . . the Publican . . .
why do I revel . . . in sinnerhood? . . . is it because . . .
I am, in fact, the angry and hurt Elder Brother? . . .
the sneering and all-knowing host? . . . the pompously
virtuous Pharisee? . . .

the very identification with the sinner-exemplars . . .
which should be so beneficial to me . . . becomes
the stampede hysteria of my willingness . . .
eagerness . . . to judge . . . strangely . . . my savage
condemnations . . . are not the result of virtue
neo-triumphant . . . but, eternal Three within me . . .

it seems that what should be the healthy recollection
. . . of my sinful state . . . is unconsciously . . .
neurotically? . . . twisted into a sadomaniac obsession
. . . with my sins . . . an obsession that I feel
compelled to escape from . . . and the escape? . . .

pointing the condemnatory finger at others . . .
throwing enough stones . . . so that the shattering of
glass . . . in other people's houses . . . will distract
passersby . . . from looking into mine . . . scrupulously
tabulating the faults of others . . . so that my own . . .
will not be tallied . . . can the remembrance of my
sinful condition . . . God within me . . . be such an
unrecognized self-betrayal . . . that I become . . .
sin-oriented . . . and forget You . . . within me? . . .

and it's not just other people's *sins* . . . that I trumpet
with indignation, righteous and impersonal . . . it's
any behavior . . . that *I* choose to consider deviant . . .
unusual . . . it's anything that is not customary . . .
proper . . . according to established procedure . . .
that is not of the Cult of the Sanctioned . . . the *act*
itself may be totally neutral . . . but, with the
innocence of the diplomat, I supply the context . . .
that sometimes makes it read like Satan's
Handbook . . . and, of course, the more rules . . .
regulations . . . customs . . . procedures . . .
proprieties . . . observances . . . there are . . . the
more opportunities . . . for the "qualified" observer . . .
to judge . . . add to this . . . the imputation of

109

motives . . . and I can even take a *good* act . . . and
make it a horrible triumph of diabolic ingenuity . . .
a zestful crusade, indeed . . . every whack of the
righteous axe . . . a negative reinforcement . . . how
many *innocent* acts . . . torn from their context . . .
bellowed to all passersby . . . or whispered into
gulping ears! . . . what lengths will some go to . . .
in order to distract others . . . from noticing their
own sleight-of-hand insecurity? . . .

a Sister leaves the convent . . . custom and proper
procedure . . . dictate . . . that she leave . . . become a
fugitive? . . . all that she ever knew . . . and loved . . .
as a Religious . . . but she returns . . . to the scene of
departure . . . "do you know . . . that she came back . . .
and visited some of her former students . . . and in a
red dress?" . . . up to this point . . . a neutral act . . .
"it's just like her . . . and she gave the impression, no
doubt . . . that she's happier now . . . than when she
was a Religious . . . those poor children . . . were
(probably) scandalized . . . and confused" . . . the
context supplied . . . "and we know why she came
back . . . she was so unwilling to adjust to Religious
life . . . that now she's devoting all her energy to
destroying it" . . . the imputation of a motive. . . .

(in reality . . . she came back because a very
generous high school girl . . . asked her to . . .
because the young girl had confided to her . . . that she
wanted to enter Religious life . . . and now felt the

need . . . to be encouraged by the one person . . . who
still shared her private dreams. . . .)

the savage reconstruction . . . of a generous impulse . . .
of an uncircumspect Spirit-response . . . yet . . .
somehow . . . these fashion designers . . . of positive
pronouncements of uncertainties . . . seem to sleep
well . . . each night. . . .

"but you, Timothy . . . have known intimately both
what I have taught . . . and how I have lived . . .
persecution is inevitable for those who are
determined . . . to live really Christian lives . . . while
wicked and deceitful men . . . will go from bad to
worse . . . deluding others and deluding
themselves". . . .

Trinity within me . . . how many condemnations . . .
of the innocent . . . spill over from the stirred-up
bile . . . of the self-righteous! . . . You . . . Compassion
itself . . . watch . . . the priest drain the Christ-Blood . . .
count . . . the Religious pouring into their chapels . . .
view . . . the churches exgorging parents and
children every Sunday . . . yet . . . You know . . . that
even having had this contact with You . . . they can
leave You . . . in your compartment . . . comfortably . . .
and while they tick off their charitable works . . .
on the icy fingers of duty . . . they seldom advert
to their identification with You . . . Christ . . . as the
Light of the World . . . they just don't seem to

111

understand . . . that light and warmth . . . are
inseparable . . . and that there can be no warmth . . .
in self-righteous, judgmental categorizations . . .
however reinforcing to one's sense of duty
performed . . . such brazen pretensions may be. . . .

an elderly psychiatrist once said . . . that some day
we will freeze people . . . and then later . . . bring
them back to life . . . "Ladies and gentlemen" . . . he
said . . . "I've already met many of these people!" . . .

The Professional

It is so difficult . . . eternal Trinity listening to my
prayer . . . to attempt to describe . . . a person . . .
without myself falling into the very fault . . . I am
trying to expose. . . .

there is . . . the rash-judger . . . pathetic in his
unassailable righteousness . . . he appears to be the
only formidable rival . . . of Rasputin . . . for
behind-closed-doors maneuvering . . . terrifyingly
complacent . . . in his almost pathologically
planned . . . a place-in-the-sun kind of deliberate
victimization . . . he seems to be energized by
contempt . . . smooth . . . polished . . . meticulous . . .
immaculate . . . by his arrogant exploitations . . .
humble . . . obsequious . . . clay-footed . . .
he apparently deals in manageable exactitudes . . .
solemn . . . clever . . . calculating . . . the Professional
. . . programmed, as it were, to destroy . . . character
and integrity . . . according to the unrealized, perhaps,
dictates . . . of his ever-kibitzing id . . . his

bargaining? . . . in the inner chamber . . . of
repression . . . tyranny . . . threat . . . his currency? . . .
the self-exonerating question . . . "did you hear
anything about?" . . . "is it true what I heard?" . . .
"has anyone said anything to you?" . . . his
magnetism? . . . purveying the inside story . . . the
gossip cunningly disguised . . . the ultimate shock . . .
treacherously delayed . . . his cover? . . . collusion . . .
like the prosecuting attorney conspiring with the trial
judge . . . in his pious scheming . . . he teases his
audience into derisory epithets . . . he has merely
asked a question or two . . . expressed concern . . .
or, in horrified disbelief, repeated "something" he
happened to hear. . . .

on the basis of the appearances . . . of the other
person's actions . . . the Professional . . . under the
guise of "concern" . . . can . . . by pious-ridden
innuendos . . . by all the accepted "concern
bromides" . . . spread what he has judged to be . . .
"inappropriate" activity . . . moral or intellectual . . .
to others who are all too eager . . . to share his
"concern" . . . he *knows* . . . that he has insufficient
evidence . . . he *knows* . . . how his statements will be
interpreted . . . embellished in their repetition . . .
he *knows* . . . that the person he's "concerned"
about . . . may well be destroyed . . . yet he
relentlessly pursues . . . Trinity within . . . may he
be psychopathic . . . thereby not responsible! . . .
what is there is . . . a hidden, jealous resentment . . .
that motivates him? . . . (the reason we give . . . and

114

the real one?) . . . his motives are unimportant . . .
this "case" has nothing to do with his personal
feelings . . . what *is* important . . . is that this
person . . . must be corrected . . . the Professional is
well aware . . . that authority doesn't generally
create . . . an atmosphere of universal approval . . .
and, therefore, authority is vulnerable . . . he knows . . .
the proper button to push . . . to set the mechanism of
disapproval in motion . . . capitalizing on this
vulnerability . . . in fact . . . sometimes authority will
bestow . . . a stray ray of limelight. . . .

so . . . the Professional informs everyone of his
"concern" . . . everyone . . . but the person involved! . . .
and by the time . . . this "concern" reaches the proper
authorities . . . the information reads like
something . . . that would be banned . . . in the
office of the Devil's Advocate. . . .

perhaps, eternal Three within us . . . an
overstatement? . . . to everyone but the victim . . .
such a Professional . . . does not . . . cannot . . .
exist?. . . how sincere . . . or psychologically
dislocated . . . was the man who thanked You . . .
that he was not like the rest of men? . . . the
Pharisees? . . . did they know their evidence was
insufficient? . . .
. . . their statements would be interpreted
. . . and embellished? . . .
. . . the object of their "concern" would be
destroyed? . . .

115

have they all disappeared? . . . is your ideal . . . of
love . . . Christ Jesus . . . no longer in tension? . . .
anyway . . . the accused is finally asked . . . to "explain
himself" . . . prove that he is innocent? . . . and, even if
he should . . . there may always be the cloud of
guilt . . . at least the mist . . . of suspicion. . . .

computerized character assassination. . . .

Father . . . Son . . . Spirit . . . Indwellers . . . watching
and reviewing . . . we read Paul's words to the
Thessalonians: "live together in peace . . . and our
instruction to this end . . . is to reprimand the unruly . . .
encourage the timid, help the weak . . . and be very
patient with all men" . . . how out in the open Paul
wants us to be! . . . the "good news" . . . becomes . . .
just a catalogue of nice-Nellyisms . . . when treachery
supplants candor . . . secretiveness . . . tiptoes by
openness . . . rationalization closes the shutter . . . on
self-revelation . . . and if there is even so much as a
scrambled hint . . . that authority . . . will inflate . . .
the original stealthy moralizings on the "inappropriate"
behavior . . . into dogmatic denunciations . . . (guilt
by hearsay) . . . then the good news . . . is bad news . . .
downright . . . and unbridled. . . .

You . . . the Judge . . . watching us . . . hoisting
ourselves into your place . . . or to where You're
supposed to be . . . how can there be so much
christened insecurity? . . . that we must damn others . . .

in order to sanctify ourselves? . . . how saved we feel! . . . could this "concern" . . . be like the "self-inspired efforts" . . . Paul speaks about . . . the "policy of self-humbling" . . . the "studied neglect of the body" . . . which in practice "do honor . . . not to God . . . but to man's own pride"? . . . why . . . when You extend to us . . . a ladder of mercy and forgiveness . . . do we, in turn, insist . . . on building a tower . . . of "concern" that is but jealousy . . . of "consultation" that is but gossip . . . of "observation" that is but prejudgment? . . .

a vigilante justice . . . implemented to release private vengeance. . . .

Person-Ache

Once I heard a priest exclaim . . . "I was a person
long before I was a priest!" . . . a despairing cry of
frustration? . . . or a horrible indictment? . . . or a
plea? . . . whatever . . . it would seem that it may be a
key to unlock the door . . . to the feelings of
discomfiture . . . loneliness . . . uselessness . . .
identity-loss . . . in a word . . . depersonalization . . .
if we . . . Father, Son, Spirit . . . began to respect
the person . . . of each somebody we meet . . . a respect
that sheds . . . once and for all . . . the smug
omniscience . . . of a Psych. I course . . . the basis of
so many of our judgments. . . .

if we began to respect . . . in the sense of trying to
understand a person . . . from his own point of view . . .
his history . . . the significance he gives to his
experiences . . . his desires as he describes them . . . if
we tried to see the person . . . as he sees himself . . .
then, eternal Three . . . our "understanding" . . . would
not be the composite . . . of our many shrewd

119

analyses . . . cold . . . distant . . . detached . . . of that
person's weaknesses only . . . rather . . . respect and
understanding . . . would demand that this person's
perceptions . . . his convictions . . . his values . . . be
conveyed only by him . . . that his ideas . . . his
feelings . . . his attitudes . . . are most validly
related . . . by him himself. . . .

respect . . . further demands . . . that we accept what
he tells us . . . then . . . Triune God within us . . . we
would have to be most hesitant to judge . . . especially,
as we often do, by projecting . . . our own
environmental prejudices . . . or personality
disorders . . . his otherness . . . would be too sacred . . .
to see it in terms of anyone else . . . but himself. . . .

we above all . . . who believe that You dwell . . .
within us . . . we should be the first . . . to recognize
the value . . . the pricelessness . . . of each person . . .
the problem? . . . not having grasped . . . interpersonal
relations . . . in meaning . . . in challenge . . . in
self-realization . . . in diversity but not
incompatibility. . . .

either . . .

we observe a person . . . from a pinnacle . . .
intellectual or moral . . . instead of having a feeling
for him . . . an awareness . . . a sensing of him . . .
we care for him . . . but do we experience him? . . . the

trivialities . . . of gray manners . . . always surface . . .
an agnostic neutrality . . . toward his value . . . as
preternatural analysts . . . with a "divine"
commission . . . to reject all those parts of him . . .
not yet absolute in their perfection . . . instead of
realizing that we cannot separate him . . . from his
parts . . . desires, plans, weaknesses, ideals, successes,
failures . . . dreams . . . that he exists . . . as a whole . . .
that to judge and reject . . . any of his significant
aspects is to reject . . . him . . . as a whole . . . as
unique . . . as sacred . . . as desirous of belonging . . .
of being loved . . . accepted . . . identified . . . with the
elusive yet final verdict . . . Christ-man. . . .

or . . .

interpersonal relations are hindered . . . really
never begun? . . . because when we talk about
charity . . . kindness . . . patience . . . when we
examine ourselves with regard to . . . relating to
others . . . or to the sacredness of a person . . . or to
the turmoil called people . . . or to our lack of
sincerity . . . thoughtfulness . . . compassion . . . we
seem to look upon all these . . . as *things* . . . things
which must be done . . . things in themselves . . .
things lacking to our sanctity . . . things needed for
our moral well-being . . . no interpersonal context . . .
charity . . . or patience . . . or compassion . . . or
self-sacrifice . . . as means of relating to others . . .
but things as in points for consideration . . . as in

121

resolutions . . . as in ejaculatory prayer . . . how far
from . . . the really vital . . . human . . . context . . . of
relating . . . in awe and wonder . . . with the possibility
of improving these means . . . deepening this
relationship . . . being present as a genuine self . . . to
the wholeness of this other person. . . .

in full communion. . . .

and since we persist . . . in pursuing . . . a
thing-morality . . . in looking upon these virtues . . .
interpersonal in nature . . . as things to be done *to*
others . . . from a safe and protected distance . . .
without involvement . . . we eventually . . . consciously
or not . . . come to look upon persons . . . as things! . . .
I do this *thing* called virtue . . . to or for that thing
called person . . . to procure for myself . . . the thing
called merit . . . thus to increase the thing . . . called
holiness . . . we seldom realize . . . that our stilted
preoccupation with the preservation of the
thingness . . . of our ascetical busy-work . . . stifles
the creative building of dynamic human
relationships . . . that our prayers and sacrifices . . .
have a definite relation to the people around us . . .
and until we do understand . . . this relationship . . .
your identification, Christ . . . will mean little to
us . . . even nothing . . . and the simplicity . . . the
effortlessness: take this unidentified thing . . . judge
and condemn it . . . it's not that easy . . . when we are
dealing with . . . an identified person! . . .

it seems . . . that this is one of the reasons . . . why there can be people . . . who are genuine perfectionists . . . when it comes to fulfilling their duties . . . their obligations . . . living according to all the proper procedures . . . acting always with propriety . . . performing as is expected of their roles . . . and yet . . . totally unaware . . . even unconcerned . . . about the persons with whom they come into contact . . . they are just things . . . to be manipulated . . . for better or worse . . . according to the convenient criteria of my needs . . . my motives . . . be they material . . . or spiritual . . . real or imagined . . . sincere or rationalized . . . and all this . . . within my own personal . . . private . . . meticulously constructed Thingdom. . . .

Up from Slavery

If we do identify people at all . . . it is as "cases" . . .
cases are things. . . .

legalism . . . that comfortable slavery . . . of
noncreative, mechanical rule-keeping . . . which
inflates trivial and scrupulous observance . . .
and . . . flattens the magnificent . . . the God-given . . .
which is You yourself . . . within us . . . legalism . . .
the data processing of mounds of minute
regulations . . . divided and subdivided . . . by which
we can pass judgment . . . and sentence . . . having
been suckled ourselves . . . on the fictions of
unrestrained casuistry . . . trained to the overkill of
detailed moralizing . . . in our own cases . . . we find
ourselves . . . more frequently than not . . . observing
others . . . not as *they* are . . . but as *we* are . . .
legalistic projection . . . transferring our own distorted
perception of law . . . to the actions of those around
us . . . our own mastery of moral trivia . . . to the
tiniest squirmings of others . . . and so . . . almost

125

each person . . . becomes a "case" . . . that we
examine . . . with bespectacled dedication . . . the
wonder that is each human being . . . is viewed . . .
with heavy-eyed boredom . . . only his faults . . .
failings . . . shortcomings . . . imperfections . . . his
being "different" . . . awaken our interest . . . our
obsessive-compulsive worriment . . . over moralistic
incidentals . . . leaves us . . . little freedom . . . to
internalize anything but the kind of rectitude . . .
that prowls around . . . looking for confrontations . . .
leaves us . . . few moments . . . to cultivate a
nonjuridic, compassionate outlook on others. . . .

well-learned legalistic anthropomorphism . . . helps
me to reduce You . . . God . . . to a stern, unbending,
heartless, shortsighted . . . Lawgiver . . . to a whimsical,
senile, capricious . . . Judge . . . avenging . . . just
waiting for me to "break the law" . . . so You can
judge me . . . and condemn me . . . and if I want to be
perfect . . . as You are . . . Father within me . . . I must
carry with me . . . the ledger of legalisms . . . checking
off the moral . . . minuses and pluses . . . on the balance
sheet . . . of each and every "case" . . . then, indeed, I
shall be . . . "God-like" . . . my legalistic training . . .
comes through . . . most accurately . . . when I'm
dealing with others . . these "cases" . . . and if others
want to strive for perfection . . . my education tells
me . . . they must be faultless . . . otherwise . . . I must
render judgment upon them . . . my thorough

legalistic indoctrination . . . tells me . . . that You are
a Lofty Lover . . . and if I am to be perfect as You . . .
I must preserve myself . . . from involvement . . . so
that I can judge all equally before . . . our law . . .
yours and mine . . . my lessons have been learned
well . . . I've made the grade . . . I enjoy being your
unofficial nay-sayer . . . legalism . . . has contributed
substantially . . . to my achievements . . . in rash
judgment. . . .

is it any wonder . . . that the Gospel tension . . .
has been described as . . . being between concern . . .
and indifference! . . . (the priest . . . and the Levite . . .
were not accused . . . of perpetrating the evil . . . of
beating and robbing . . . the traveler! . . .) St. Paul
teaches . . . that if I give away everything I have . . .
and don't have Charity . . . I achieve precisely
nothing . . . in other words . . . I can do a lot of
things . . . even the extreme thing . . . of giving my
body over to be burned . . . but if it's not in an
interpersonal context . . . if what I do . . . doesn't have
a relationship to other people . . . (Charity) . . . then . . .
all these *things* . . . total up to zero. . . .

moreover . . . these things can produce . . . a fattened
righteousness . . . they're so easily measured . . . my
personal sacrifices . . . my external poverty (usually
by vow) . . . the *time* spent in saying my prayers . . .
all measurable . . . in my own life . . . and in the lives

127

of others? . . . any degree of absence . . . of these
things . . . offers me the opportunity . . . to don the
solemn robes . . . of presiding judge. . . .

likewise . . . I will convene my court . . . whenever
I find someone . . . who in his deep concern for
people . . . may from time to time . . . bypass some
arbitrary rules . . . or canonized customs . . . or frozen
proprieties . . . and I will ignore the fact . . . in my
eagerness to sentence him . . . that his actions are
dictated by a very true interpersonal regard . . . for
others . . . and my condemnation . . . will issue forth
from my unconsciousness of . . . or my unwillingness
to admit . . . the real needs of real people . . . ("I've
performed my duty . . . now let them take it or leave
it" . . . "I've fulfilled my obligation . . . now it's up to
them") . . . and if the defendant . . . in my court . . .
is guilty of nothing . . . I can always help him . . .
experience guilt . . . by accusing him of . . .
imprudence! . . .

the tragedy: the norm for his imprudence . . . is his
lack of concern for the "proper procedure" . . .
arbitrarily . . . subjectively . . . legalistically . . .
established . . . by me! . . . I am sorely unaware . . .
that, in effect, I am saying "it doesn't matter that
someone . . . goes unaided . . . as long as we stay
within the bounds of propriety" . . . or at least . . .
in effect . . . "we will help . . . as long as our aid . . .
doesn't force us to overstep . . . the 'prudent'

limits . . . set down by time-honored custom . . . or
commonly accepted images" . . . or, in fact, I am
saying . . . "we don't like your attitude" . . . (terminally
punctuated). . . .

You, Christ . . . gave us . . . a thrust ethic . . .
why, then, do we demand . . . of *others* . . .
righteous-behavioral totalism . . . every act of
man-as-moral . . . must equal absolute perfection? . . .
while in our own case . . . it's a "mirror-mirror-on-
the-wall" morality. . . .

Concern: Two Life-Styles

Certainly . . . at times concern may seem wild and
impetuous . . . but it may also be . . . imaginative
and creative . . . (You . . . Spirit . . . are creative . . .
and creativity can be most disruptive) . . . certainly . . .
there are proper channels . . . as long as they are not
used . . . as excuses for interpersonal inertia . . . as
long as they do not become . . . idols . . . absorbing
our concentrated worship . . . to the extent that we
become oblivious . . . of the flesh-and-blood reality . . .
of human needs. . . .

Father . . . Son . . . and Spirit . . . concern for the needs
of others . . . can drain us . . . time . . . energy . . .
patience . . . imaginative planning . . . health . . .
peace . . . and in return? . . . frustration . . .
thanklessness . . . feeling "used" . . . indifference . . .
condescending criticism from our fellow workers . . .
the obvious temptation . . . is to look for ways to
rationalize ourselves into safe . . . even "virtuous" . . .
niches . . . of "procedure" . . . or "custom" . . . and in

order to reinforce . . . our rationalization . . . we feel
compelled to condemn those . . . who refuse to find
their niche . . . who have indeed dared to be
different . . . who do not conform . . . who do not
play it safe . . . whose scissors of concern . . . cut
through the red tape of propriety . . . that they may
get to where . . . it must happen . . . to where the
needs are . . . to where the action cannot be handled . . .
by the perfunctorily religious . . . while *we* wait . . .
for the red tape . . . to be showered . . . like ticker
tape . . . upon our "good-and-faithful-servant"
disregard . . . for the destitution of our fellowmen. . . .

equal emphasis! . . . those who stoke the inner fires
of intense concern . . . for others in need . . . must not
flagrantly . . . nor arbitrarily . . . let their burning zeal
gut . . . the structure of rules . . . regulations . . . duties
and obligations . . . they must make certain . . . that
they are responding . . . to your promptings . . .
Holy Spirit . . . and not just to their own neurotic
need . . . for the limelight . . . or to their unrecognized
desire . . . for liberation from a literalistic legal
mentality . . . through the instant therapy . . . of
social involvement . . . those . . . on the other hand . . .
who uphold the rubric of duty . . . as supreme . . .
must be on their guard . . . lest they drop only
scraps . . . from their table of prayer . . . obligation . . .
rule-keeping . . . to others in need . . . lest, in saving
themselves . . . they have little or no time . . .
energy . . . room . . . for others . . . lest they shout

down . . . your suggestions . . . Spirit of love . . . with
the very noise . . . of their own "speak, Lords". . . .

mutual help . . . that each may understand . . . at least
recognize the difference in . . . the other's perception . . .
not judge it . . . not condemn it . . . casually terrifying
one another . . . hiding behind a self-excluding
"we" . . . proper procedure is essential . . . that, in
order, more good may be done . . . more efficiently . . .
interpersonal context is essential . . . that the good
being done . . . may not be narcissistic . . .
bureaucratic . . . coldly professional . . . with care . . .
but without feeling. . . .

it seems, however . . . that custom . . . propriety . . .
proper procedure . . . carry most of the weight . . .
if, for no other reason, than that they represent . . .
what has always been done . . . what's been around
the longest . . . therefore . . . those of us who lean . . .
heavily . . . almost exclusively . . . on customary
procedure . . . conservative by instinct . . . fearful
by ideology . . . may find ourselves deviously
maneuvered . . . by a massive dose of caution . . . into
the position of judging . . . those who prefer . . . to
try something different . . . or unusual . . . or novel . . .
who are nerve-rackingly creative . . . disturbingly
innovative . . . in their approach . . . who do not look
for . . . the reward allotted . . . to excessive
conformity . . . those of us . . . who favor the "tried
and true" . . . may be the conventional victims . . .

133

of slithering hypocrisy . . . this is due . . . to our own
articulate, human imperfections . . . we will fail from
time to time . . . but because of our "customary
procedure" of judging others . . . we are forced to
wear the mask . . . of startled innocence . . . the
"who-me?" defensive perfectionism . . . thus . . . the
exclamatory perversion of the axiom . . . "it must not
only *be* right . . . it must *appear* right" . . . that is, the
eventual stuffed-soul satisfaction . . . with the
(unconscious) feeling that . . . "all's right that appears
right"! . . .

and what about this "appears right"? . . . it's
meaning? . . . does it mean . . . that we are interested
in the customary procedure . . . the proper way of
doing things . . . as people expect them to be done? . . .
does "appears right" mean . . . that we have a
preoccupied eye on those who will be judging *us*? . . .
are we, indeed, more concerned . . . about man's
judgment of us . . . than about your judgment . . .
You who observe us so intimately . . . from within? . . .
and if we do continue to be obsessed . . . with how
what we do . . . will look to others . . . will not this
obsession restrict your activity within us . . . Spirit of
the Father and Son . . . urging us to respond to the
needs of others? . . . can our response be genuine . . .
human . . . Spirit-inflated . . . if we are excruciatingly
at pains . . . to see to it that this response of ours will
appear right . . . in the eyes of those . . . we think will
be judging us . . . according to their all-too-human

and fallible standards . . . according to how they think
our response should appear? . . . and so . . . much of
our generosity . . . spontaneous . . . joyous . . .
instantaneous . . . uninhibited . . . free . . . will, as a
matter of fact, be curtailed . . . or stifled . . . or aborted
at inception . . . or, at best . . . come forth in a
paralytic, pathetic crawl . . . uninspiring . . . pitiful . . .
circumspect . . . timid . . . fearful. . . .

a generosity . . . that is unchained from your
urgings . . . Spirit of freedom. . . .

and it may well be . . . that, because we are so
crippled and deformed . . . floundering, not free . . .
in our generosity . . . we feel compelled to sit in
judgment on those . . . who seem less concerned
about what others think . . . who are more daring . . .
in their response to others in need . . . who are bold
enough . . . to be honest . . . in evaluating their
actions . . . as *being* right . . . regardless of how these
actions appear . . . to those who are all too easily
prone . . . to judge rashly . . . anyway. . . .

Interpersonal Renewal

Father . . . Son . . . Spirit . . . You read my heart . . .
from within . . . I may appear to others . . . as the
establishment's schizophrenic iconoclast . . . creative
excursions are seldom rewarded . . . where order and
discipline . . . are highly prized . . . yet, renewal, if it's
to be at all creative . . . can flourish . . . only in an
atmosphere of acceptance . . . where it's safe to fail . . .
where the only real failure . . . is not to try at all. . . .

iconoclasm? . . .

not quite . . . just a plea . . . to outmaneuver the efforts
of fuddy-duddyism . . . to keep customs . . . proper
procedures . . . bureaucratic channels . . . flexible
enough . . . that change is not only made possible . . .
rather, built-in . . . obviously . . . there's a difference . . .
between your unchangeable laws . . . and the
changeable customs of man . . . but why the aura of
divinity . . . about man-made rules? . . . but why the
canonization of anachronistic customs? . . . the

inflexibility? . . . so that any deviation is regarded as
heresy . . . at least . . . disloyalty . . . so that a free
spirit . . . creative and innovative . . . must be the
maverick? . . . in any given custom . . . there should
be room . . . flexibility . . . not for exceptions . . . but
for pre-planned ways of doing things differently . . .
all customs must respect individual differences . . . if
this respect were activated . . . there would be far
fewer opportunities . . . for anyone to judge . . .
custom that reduces . . . each sacred human being . . .
to an interchangeable part . . . that fears, distrusts,
dislikes . . . diversity . . . that designs a melting pot . . .
(which, in fact, is a powder keg) . . . to mix all
differences out of existence . . . that is organized . . .
to turn out . . . a standardized product . . . the
cliché-man . . . such custom merely provides . . .
myriads of peepholes . . . for judgmental scrutinies . . .
and all this . . . in areas that have nothing to do
with . . . morality . . . so often. . . .

sadly . . . we who swagger onto your Judgment
Seat . . . God within us . . . make so certain that we
are insulated from outside scrutiny . . . protected
from honest introspection . . . that the real motive for
our judgments . . . envy . . . becomes so beclouded . .
that that, in itself, is cause for others . . . to judge
us . . . the literal vicious circle! . . . maliciously
repeated . . . a spinning medley . . . in our pervasive
self-delusion . . . we, in the meantime, produce all

kinds of good and holy motives . . . protest our
detachment . . . proclaim our desire that no harm be
done. . . .

why . . . when we congregate in the splendor of
authority . . . can't we (and authority) . . . presume
innocence . . . really . . . not just verbally . . . instead
of guilt . . . sincerity . . . instead of ulterior
motives . . . prudence instead of imprudence . . .
both accurately defined! . . . a desire to help . . . instead
of a plot to disturb . . . honesty instead of deception . . .
thoughtfulness . . . instead of ambition . . . why don't
we try to make excuses *for* people . . . instead of
fabricating cases against people? . . . why not
exonerate . . . rather than condemn? . . . could
it be . . . that in imputing unworthy motives . . .
self-seeking manipulations . . . to others . . . we are, in
effect . . . projecting our own attitudes . . . motives . . .
values . . . ambitious designs . . . self-aggrandizing
gestures . . . to others? . . . that in our scrupulous
efforts . . . to judge others . . . we are unwittingly
revealing ourselves . . . even to the most amateur
psychological eye . . . what is basest . . . meanest . . .
most selfish . . . lowest . . . in ourselves? . . . that all the
vices we "find" in others . . . are really our own? . . .
all the while . . . thinking we are shrewdly getting
away with something . . . a something . . . that exposes
us . . . even to the casual eye . . . not to mention . . .
the searching eye. . . .

139

renewal? . . . and all the talk about updating? . . .
what does it mean? . . . oversimplifying is
hazardous . . . but aren't we seeking better means . . .
to express our interpersonal concern for current
needs . . . and present problems . . . as well as looking
for . . . now . . . healing persons as remedies for
"future shock"? . . . that disease . . . which is a time
phenomenon . . . the product of the greatly
accelerated rate . . . of change in society . . . causing
a dizzying disorientation . . . so that there are no
familiar clues . . . a breakdown in communication . . .
a misreading of reality . . . an inability to cope . . . (so
Alvin Toffler sees it). . . .

the popular voice cries . . . "the world's going
mad!" . . .

Trinity within us all . . . the symptoms are all around
us . . . hair lengths . . . cool . . . encounter . . .
activism . . . protests . . . nudity . . . backlash . . .
permissiveness . . . violence . . . prejudice . . .
alienation . . . peace . . . pot . . . lib . . . love . . . serious
symptoms . . . eternal Three within me . . . demanding
interpersonal renewal. . . .

yet . . . because of all the individual contributions . . .
to the overall impact of rash judgment . . . it would
seem that we should make certain . . . in the first

140

place . . . that some genuine interpersonal concern
exists! . . . at all . . . an interpersonal concern . . . that
can be brought up to date . . . into focus . . .
renewed . . . the raw material . . . must preexist . . .
any refinement . . . judgment . . . that's rash . . .
without proof . . . based on an individual's
closed-minded interpretation . . . of the facts and the
circumstances . . . negates true interpersonal
concern . . . and the renewal? . . . it could end up,
as someone pointed out . . . as mere ecclesiastical
furniture shuffling . . . changes that are but awkward
and wooden adjustments . . . a new format that is a
new rigidity . . . a different procedure for implementing
the same old thing . . . rendering us the laughing-
stocks of posterity . . . (something about new wine
and old wineskins?) . . . perhaps. . . .

as long as we persist . . . in negating interpersonal
concern . . . with our slanted and hasty judgments . . .
baseless . . . we can expect . . . the advocates of
renewal . . . honest, sincere and pulsating with
devotion to your church . . . Christ-Brother . . . to
become less and less willing . . . to reveal their true
and imperfect communications . . . especially if they
do disagree with the "official" position . . . or the
honored modus agendi . . . or the prudent position . . .
in fact, why is it . . . when someone wants sincerely
to try to communicate . . . what he really thinks and
feels . . . viewpoints differing from our perception . . .

141

he is judged as obstinate or brash . . . ignorant or
radical . . . disloyal or subversive? . . . ("that man
has a problem!") . . . .

isn't it possible . . . that he merely and *sincerely*
wants to let another human being know . . . just what
is going on within him . . . with all the accompanying
anguish . . . or fear . . . or anxiety . . . or hope? . . .
but, because he is judged so rapidly . . . condemned
so righteously . . . he is turned off . . . forced to live
his life in order to impress others . . . rather than
to express himself. . . .

and the renewal . . . while being hospitably
entertained . . . in synods . . . committees . . . senates . . .
chapters . . . advisory councils . . . may be turned out
into the cold . . . by the populace . . . because it may
not be taking place at the grass-roots level . . .
between persons . . . unadvocated . . . at
heart-depths . . . because there seems to be no united
effort . . . of many individuals . . . to produce a
general climate of candor . . . maintaining a steady . . .
unalarmed . . . openness . . . unencumbered by tired
and trivial phrases . . . revealing themselves . . .
striving for freshly ambitioned understanding . . .
mutual . . . circumspect to the point of deferring
judgments . . . prudently uncondemning . . . accessible
to fresh perspectives . . . responsive to the tug of new
facts . . . fiercely hesitant about circumstantial

evidence . . . renewal . . . at heart-level . . . goes whole
Lamb . . . not to judge! . . .

You, Christ-Victim . . . as a matter of recorded fact . . .
were condemned . . . and to death . . . because You
spoke out . . . honestly . . . against the man-made
customs . . . even the Pharisee-imposed laws . . . of
your day . . . ironically . . . there seems to be no
evidence that the groups against You . . . went to their
graves . . . thinking they were not justified . . . never
doubting that they were not vindicated . . . in your
crucifixion . . . death . . . even their controlled
contempt . . . and persecution of those who preached
your resurrection . . . was an attempt to prove . . .
that their judgment had been right . . . all along . . .
that their condemnation . . . had been justifiable . . .
from the start . . . your condemnation . . . will, for
all days . . . stand as a condemnation . . . of those who
would rather see the person broken . . . than the law . . .
however. . . .

Conclusion or the Ongoing?

Perhaps in the final analysis . . . having realized
through many bitter experiences . . . the fact that
no matter how bravely . . . we strive for the ideal of
charity . . . love . . . genuine interpersonal
renewal . . . concern . . . we will eventually . . .
ultimately . . . be disappointed . . . that man will
forever be . . . man's chief predator . . . conflict . . .
struggle . . . aggression . . . revenge . . . hatred . . .
war . . . the desire to humiliate . . . through rash
judgments . . . equal something savage . . . even in
pacifism . . . even in loyalty . . . and perhaps . . .
having come to this conclusion . . . we are driven
back to You . . . Trinity within us . . . recognizing
that You . . . are Stability itself . . . You are
Dependability itself . . . whose judgments . . . alone . . .
are truly all-knowing . . . all-loving . . . as well as
just . . . that You . . . want and desire and will . . .
the salvation of each of us . . . within us . . . this
return to You . . . Father, Son and Spirit . . . Trinity . . .
within . . . an escape? . . . a serene "no" . . . to my

fellow man? . . . an opium . . . to help me forget . . .
my disappointment in him? . . .

rather . . . a sign . . . a radiation . . . that You alone
will not fail . . . that You are always faithful. . . .

escapism? . . . not if we understand . . . that it is only
through the bitterness of disappointment . . . in the
weakness . . . undependability . . . proneness to
judge . . . readiness to condemn . . . found in such
abundance . . . in our fellow man . . . that we will
find . . . after we look for it . . . your strength . . .
your dependability . . . your encouragement . . . your
willingness to give still another chance . . . your
patient teaching. . . .

escapism? . . . hardly . . . because we know . . . that
we, too, share . . . in the very same weakness . . . the
very same instability . . . that we, too, are guilty . . .
I am guilty! . . . of the same kinds of judgments . . . that
rip my own heart . . . to shreds . . . when they are
perpetrated against me . . . that I am just as guilty . . .
of those condemnations . . . without sufficient
evidence . . . as the ones I point out in others . . .
that . . . while I decry those . . . who would judge on
appearances only . . . who would impute motives to
others . . . who would live in lavish righteousness . . .
posed . . . as "sainted survivors" . . . of traditional
maxims . . . I must admit . . . I am just as guilty . . .
guiltier . . . and it is this realization . . . that forces

146

me to seek You . . . to find . . . and the wonder . . . the
tantalizing mystery . . . the violent logic . . . alarming
in its reasoning . . . bewildering . . . in its
conclusion . . . You are there . . . *here* . . . right within
me! . . . waiting . . . inviting . . . wanting me to seek
You in. . . .

out of my everymannish disappointment . . . You
teach me . . . that in all the judgments . . . against
me . . . that shatter my heart . . . that shove me off
the edge of panic . . . into the dizzying depths . . . of
despondency . . . that out of my exponential
discouragement . . . with myself . . . in all the
judgments . . . I construe about others . . . cruel . . .
snide . . . offhanded . . . debilitating . . .
unreasonable . . . witty . . . You teach me . . . within . . .
that You and You alone . . . are Judge . . . not some
faceless, unreachable . . . remote, petty . . . pompous,
mindless . . . menacing, wanton . . . detached,
disinterested . . . judge . . . but a Judge . . . who
loves . . . enough . . . to share your life . . . with me . . .
to dwell within me . . . I believe this . . . or I believe
nothing . . . Father . . . Son . . . Spirit . . . Indwellers. . . .

escapism? . . .

to return to You . . . within me? . . . hardly . . . because
your challenge . . . Jesus-Teacher . . . remains . . .
to maintain faith in people . . . despite their
judgments . . . their pettiness . . . their preoccupation

with neutral trivia . . . their empty-minded forays . . .
into the sacred precincts of another's fragile
conscience . . . even to hurt . . . destroy . . .
realizing . . . their sinful condition . . . yet Indwelt . . .
I come to You . . . Trinity within me . . . here to be
strengthened . . . only that I might go back . . . among
men . . . to them . . . bringing them your love . . .
fused with my own . . . and, since You first loved
me . . . when I was urgently unlovable . . . I can
love . . . as You love . . . because . . . the oftener I
find people . . . unlovable . . . in their judgments . . .
righteous anger . . . condemnation . . . spiritual
pride . . . prying rectitude . . . the more
opportunities . . . I have . . . to express to them . . .
share with them . . . your kind of love . . .
indwelling. . . .

Amen.